DISCIPLESPATH

W9-DET-832

THE
LIFE

LIVING THE SPIRITUAL
DISCIPLINES

LifeWay Press®
Nashville, Tennessee

✛DISCIPLES PATH

Disciples Path is a series of studies founded on Jesus' model of discipleship. Created by experienced disciple makers across the nation, it offers an intentional pathway for transformational discipleship and a way to help followers of Christ move from new disciples to mature disciple makers. Each study in the series is built on the principles of modeling, practicing, and multiplying:

- Leaders model the life of a biblical disciple.

- Disciples follow and practice from the leader.

- Disciples become disciple makers and multiply through the *Disciples Path*.

Each study in the series has been written and approved by disciple-makers for small groups and one-on-one settings.

Contributors:

Carolyn Taketa, Calvary Community Church, Westlake Village, CA
Drew Sams, Bel Aire Presbyterian Church, Los Angeles, CA

MINISTRY GRID
training made simple

For helps on how to use *Disciples Path,* tips on how to better lead groups, or additional ideas for leading this study, visit: *ministrygrid.com/web/disciplespath*

Item: 005717354 • ISBN: 978-1-4300-3954-9
Dewey decimal classification number: 248.684
Subject heading: DISCIPLESHIP \ GOD \ CHRISTIAN LIFE

Eric Geiger
Vice President, LifeWay Resources

Rick Howerton
Discipleship Specialist

Sam O'Neal, Joel Polk
Content Editors

Brian Daniel
Manager, Discipleship Publishing

Michael Kelley
Director, Groups Ministry

We believe that the Bible has God for its author; salvation for its end; and truth, without any mixture of error, for its matter and that all Scripture is totally true and trustworthy. To review LifeWay's doctrinal guideline, visit *lifeway.com/doctrinalguideline.*

Unless otherwise noted, all Scripture quotations are taken from the Holman Christian Standard Bible®, copyright 1999, 2000, 2002, 2003, 2009 by Holman Bible Publishers. Used by permission. Scripture quotations marked NIV are taken from the Holy Bible, NEW INTERNATIONAL VERSION®. Copyright © 1973, 1978, 1984 by Biblica, Inc. All rights reserved worldwide. Used by permission. Scripture quotations marked (NLT) are taken from the Holy Bible, New Living Translation, copyright © 1996. Used by permission of Tyndale House Publishers, Inc., Wheaton, IL 60189 USA. All rights reserved. Scripture quotations marked (ESV) are from The Holy Bible, English Standard Version® (ESV®), copyright © 2001 by Crossway, a publishing ministry of Good News Publishers. Used by permission. All rights reserved.

To order additional copies of this resource, write to LifeWay Resources Customer Service; One LifeWay Plaza; Nashville, TN 37234-0113; fax 615.251.5933; call toll free 800.458.2772; order online at *lifeway.com;* email *orderentry@lifeway.com;* or visit the LifeWay Christian Store serving you.

Printed in the United States of America

Groups Ministry Publishing, LifeWay Resources
One LifeWay Plaza; Nashville, TN 37234-0152

CONTENTS

A NOTE FOR DISCIPLE MAKERS

Several years ago I was part of a massive research study that sought to discover how the Lord often brings about transformation in the hearts of His people. The study became a book called *Transformational Discipleship*. Basically, we wanted to learn how disciples are made. Based on the study of Scripture and lots of interactions with people, we concluded that transformation is likely to occur when a godly **leader** applies **truth** to the heart of a person while that person is in a teachable **posture.**

- **LEADER:** You are the leader. As you invest in the people you're discipling, they will learn much about the Christian faith by watching you, by sensing your heart for the Lord, and by seeing you pursue Him. I encourage you to seek to be the type of leader who can say, "Follow my example as I follow the example of Christ."

- **TRUTH:** All six studies in the *Disciples Path* series were developed in deep collaboration with ministry leaders who regularly and effectively disciple people. The studies are designed to take the people you disciple into the Word of God—because we're confident that Jesus and His Word sanctify us and transform us. Our community of disciple-makers mapped out a path of the truths we believe are essential for each believer to know and understand.

- **POSTURE:** Hopefully the people you will be investing in adopt a teachable posture—one that is open and hungry for the Lord. Encourage them to take the study seriously and to view your invitation to study together as a sacred opportunity to experience the grace of God and the truth of God.

We hope and pray the Lord will use this study in your life and the lives of those you disciple. As you apply the truth of God to teachable hearts, transformation will occur. Thank you for being a disciple-maker!

In Christ,

Eric

Eric Geiger
Vice President at LifeWay Christian Resources
Co-author of *Transformational Discipleship*

WHAT IS A DISCIPLE?

Congratulations! If you've chosen to live as a disciple of Jesus, you've made the most important decision imaginable. But you may be wondering, *What does it mean to be a disciple?*

To put it simply, a disciple of Jesus is someone who has chosen to follow Jesus. That's the command Jesus gave to those He recruited as His first disciples: "Follow Me." In Jesus' culture, religious leaders called rabbis would gather a group of followers called disciples to follow in their footsteps and learn their teachings. In the same way, you will become more and more like Jesus as you purposefully follow Him in the weeks to come. Jesus once said, "Everyone who is fully trained will be like his teacher" (Luke 6:40).

On a deeper level, disciples of Jesus are those learning to base their identities on Jesus Himself. All of us use different labels to describe who we are at the core levels of our hearts. Some think of themselves as athletes or intellectuals. Others think of themselves as professionals, parents, leaders, class clowns, and so on.

Disciples of Jesus set aside those labels and base their identities on Him. For example:

- **A disciple of Jesus is a child of God.** In the Bible we find these words: "Look at how great a love the Father has given us that we should be called God's children. And we are!" (1 John 3:1). We are God's children. He loves us as our perfect Father.

- **A disciple of Jesus is an alien in this world.** Disciples of Jesus are aliens, or outsiders, in their own cultures. Because of this identity, Jesus' disciples abstain from actions and activities that are contrary to Him. Peter, one of Jesus' original disciples, wrote these words: "Dear friends, I urge you as strangers and temporary residents to abstain from fleshly desires that war against you" (1 Pet. 2:11).

- **A disciple of Jesus is an ambassador for Christ.** Another of Jesus' disciples recorded these words in the Bible: "Therefore, if anyone is in Christ, he is a new creation; old things have passed away, and look, new things have come. … Therefore, we are ambassadors for Christ, certain that God is appealing through us. We plead on Christ's behalf, 'Be reconciled to God'" (2 Cor. 5:17,20). Ambassadors represent their king and country in a different culture for a specified period of time. Because we have been transformed by Jesus and are now His disciples and ambassadors, we represent Him to the world through our actions and by telling others about Him.

The journey you are about to take is one that will transform you more and more to be like Jesus. Enjoy! No one ever loved and cared for people more passionately than Jesus. No one was ever more sincere in His concern for others than Jesus. And no one ever gave more so that we could experience His love than Jesus did on the cross.

As you grow to be more like Jesus, you'll find that your relationships are stronger, you have more inner peace than ever before, and you look forward to the future as never before.

That's the blessing of living as a disciple of Jesus.

HOW TO USE THIS RESOURCE

Welcome to *The Life*. By exploring the journey of Jesus' earliest disciples, both new and established Christians will gain a better understanding of what it means to follow Christ. As you get started, consider the following guides and suggestions for making the most of this experience.

GROUP DISCUSSION

Because the process of discipleship always involves at least two people—the leader and the disciple—each session of *The Life* includes a practical plan for group engagement and discussion.

This plan includes the following steps:

- **GET STARTED.** The first section of the group material helps you ease into the discussion by starting on common ground. You'll begin by reflecting on the previous session and your recent experiences as a disciple. After spending time in prayer, you'll find a practical illustration to help you launch into the main topic of the current session.

- **THE STORY.** While using *Disciples Path*, you'll find opportunities to engage the Bible through both story and teaching. That's why the group time for each session features two main sections: **Know the Story** and **Unpack the Story. Know the Story** introduces a biblical text and includes follow-up questions for brief discussion. It's recommended that your group encounter the biblical text by reading it out loud. **Unpack the Story** includes practical teaching material and discussion questions—both designed to help you engage the truths contained in the biblical text. To make the most of your experience, use the provided material as a launching point for deeper conversation. As you read through the teaching material and engage the questions as a group, be thinking of how the truths you're exploring will impact your everyday life.

- **ENGAGE.** The group portion of each session ends with an activity designed to help you practice the biblical principles introduced in **Know the Story** and more fully explored in **Unpack the Story.** This part of the group time often appeals to different learning styles and will push you to engage the text at a personal level.

INDIVIDUAL DISCOVERY

Each session of *The Life* also includes content for individual use during the time between group gatherings. This content is divided into three categories:

⬆ **Worship:** features content for worship and devotion. These activities provide opportunities for you to connect with God in meaningful ways and deepen your relationship with Him.

➡⬅ **Personal study:** features content for personal study. These pages help you gain a deeper understanding of the truths and principles explored during the group discussion.

⬅➡ **Application:** features content for practical application. These suggestions help you take action based on the information you've learned and your encounters with God.

Note: Aside from the **Reading Plan,** the content provided in the Individual Discovery portion of each session should be considered optional. You'll get the most out of your personal study by working with your group leader to create a personalized discipleship plan using the **Weekly Activities** checklist included in each session.

ADDITIONAL SUGGESTIONS

- You'll be best prepared for each group discussion or mentoring conversation if you read the session material beforehand. A serious read will serve you most effectively, but skimming the **Get Started** and **The Story** sections will also be helpful if time is limited.

- The deeper you're willing to engage in the group discussions and individual discovery each session, the more you'll benefit from those experiences. Don't hold back, and don't be afraid to ask questions whenever necessary.

- As you explore the **Engage** portion of each session, you'll have the chance to practice different activities and spiritual disciplines. Take advantage of the chance to observe others during the group time—and to ask questions—so that you'll be prepared to incorporate these activities into your private spiritual life as well.

- Visit *lifeway.com/disciplespath* for a free PDF download that includes leader helps for *The Life* and additional resources for disciple-makers.

IMMERSED IN THE WORD

Immersing ourselves in God's Word provides the foundation for our identity and life.

GET STARTED

REFLECT

Welcome to *The Life*. The goal of this study is to help you answer the question, "What does a disciple *do* as a follower of Jesus?" Throughout the following sessions, we'll examine how disciples of Jesus imitate Him by immersing themselves in God's Word, remaining connected to God through prayer, living in community with other believers, understanding how a Spirit-filled life can lead to transformation, serving others for the advancement of His kingdom, and using their lives to spread the gospel into the world. In this session, we'll begin by discovering Jesus' approach to Scripture as God's Holy Word and practical steps we can take to imitate Him in this activity.

Which element in the description of the study above are you most excited about? Why?

How can a better understanding of spiritual disciplines strengthen our relationship with God and increase our ability to participate in His redemptive purposes in the world?

PRAY

Begin the session by connecting with God through prayer. Use the following guidelines as you speak with Him:

- Ask God to open your hearts and minds to hear what He has to say through His Word today.

- Thank God for His Word, which is described as perfect, restorative, trustworthy, wise, right, clear, insightful, pure, sweet, and helpful.

- Ask God for wisdom and understanding as you seek to gain a deeper understanding of God's Word.

INTRODUCTION

Who is Jesus? Do a quick Internet search and you'll find many different answers. Some of those answers will be quite specific, while others will leave you with more questions than answers. Regardless, you're bound to land on some controversy and disagreement.

Perhaps a better way to answer this question is to go to God's Holy Word. Scripture, from the beginning of Genesis to the end of Revelation, points to Jesus. Simply put, the Bible is about Jesus. It's not about us and what we must do—it's about Jesus and what He has already done. And while of course it is crucial for Christ-followers to read the Bible, *how* we read the Bible may be even more important. John Calvin says this about reading God's Word:

> The Scriptures should be read with the aim of finding Christ in them. Whoever turns aside from this object, even though he wears himself out all his life in learning, he will never reach the knowledge of the truth.[1]

When we find Christ in Scripture we will know better how to be His followers. We will be able to communicate with Him and know who He is. And though the Bible isn't about us, we will begin to understand who we are in relation to Christ. In God's Word we find that we are both more broken than we dare let on and more loved than we dare let in. In God's Word, we find our true identities, the most authentic version of ourselves. It's only when we immerse our entire lives in God's Word that we begin to live the lives God designed and desires for us.

What have you heard others say is the primary reason to read the Bible?

How does this description of the Bible differentiate it from other books throughout history?

During this session, we will explore how we can be saturated and immersed in God's Word in a way that transforms how we see God, ourselves, and the world around us.

KNOW THE STORY

After Jesus' resurrection, Luke 24 describes the story of two disciples traveling to Emmaus. On their way, a man joined them. Unbeknown to them, this man was Jesus Himself. He asked the disciples about their conversation, and they told Him how they were troubled with Jesus' death and the news that His tomb was empty. Jesus responded in verse 25,

> 25 "How unwise and slow you are to believe in your hearts all that the prophets have spoken! 26 Didn't the Messiah have to suffer these things and enter into His glory?" 27 Then beginning with Moses and all the Prophets, He interpreted for them the things concerning Himself in all the Scriptures.
> **LUKE 24:25-27**

As they continued on their journey, Jesus reminded them of the Old Testament Scriptures and prophecies that revealed all that would happen. Jesus told the confused disciples that all of Scripture was revealing who He was. They had no reason to be troubled because He was who He said He was and accomplished what God had sent Him to accomplish.

A few verses later in the same chapter, Jesus then presented Himself before all of the confused and troubled disciples. And in the same way, Jesus encouraged them by saying,

> 44 Then He told them, "These are My words that I spoke to you while I was still with you—that everything written about Me in the Law of Moses, the Prophets, and the Psalms must be fulfilled." 45 Then He opened their minds to understand the Scriptures. 46 He also said to them, "This is what is written: The Messiah would suffer and rise from the dead the third day, 47 and repentance for forgiveness of sins would be proclaimed in His name to all the nations, beginning at Jerusalem. 48 You are witnesses of these things. 49 And look, I am sending you what My Father promised. As for you, stay in the city until you are empowered from on high."
> **LUKE 24:44-49**

What are some truths we can take away from these two passages?

UNPACK THE STORY

SCRIPTURE REVEALS JESUS

He taught them how to understand Scripture and how all of redemptive history is pieced together and culminated at the cross. In verse 27, we read that "beginning with Moses and all the Prophets, He interpreted for them the things concerning Himself in all the Scriptures" (Luke 24:27). Jesus used the Scripture to give these disciples hope in the resurrection. Jesus had previously told them that He would die and be resurrected. When He presented Himself to the disciples, He revealed that all He had taught them had come true. Jesus of Nazareth is the Lord Christ—the Son of God.

Discuss some of the events in the few days surrounding Jesus' death and resurrection. What was it that made the disciples lose hope and doubt what Jesus had taught them?

When are you most likely to lose hope or doubt what Scripture teaches? Discuss how being immersed in Scripture turns that doubt into hope?

Jesus is recorded quoting Scripture 78 times in the New Testament.

This wasn't the first time Jesus used Scripture. In Luke 4, Jesus was led out into the desert and was tempted for 40 days by God's enemy, Satan. Of the three recorded temptations, Satan attacks Jesus' identity and begins two of them with "If you are the Son of God ..." (vv. 3,9). Satan essentially dares Jesus to prove His identity by doing something amazing: turning stones to bread and jumping off the temple so the angels can catch Him. Because Jesus had immersed Himself in Scripture, He doesn't have to prove His identity to Satan. Instead, He counters each temptation with the truth of Scripture.

We see this all throughout the Gospels. Jesus knew Scripture. Even as a young boy, He learned it. He memorized it. He meditated on it. And then as an adult, He allowed it to influence His ministry in countless ways. Jesus is recorded quoting Scripture 78 times in the New Testament.

Read Psalm 119:9-16 out loud in your group. How would it affect believers' lives who meditated and hid God's Word in their hearts on a daily basis?

SCRIPTURE REVEALS WHO WE REALLY ARE

Even though all of Scripture points to Jesus—and we read it with the intention and expectation of finding Jesus in Scripture—it doesn't mean we can't find anything useful in Scripture concerning ourselves. The opposite is true. When we immerse our lives in God's Word—through faith in the living Word that is Jesus and through immersing our lives in the written Word that is the Bible—we find an unshakable identity from which our entire lives can flow. Look at how these passages describe the Scripture's usefulness in the believer's life:

> [16] All Scripture is inspired by God and is profitable for teaching, for rebuking, for correcting, for training in righteousness, [17] so that the man of God may be complete, equipped for every good work.
> **2 TIMOTHY 3:16-17**

> The word of God is living and effective and sharper than any double-edged sword, penetrating as far as the separation of soul and spirit, joints and marrow. It is able to judge the ideas and thoughts of the heart.
> **HEBREWS 4:12**

What do these verses tell you about how God's Word shapes us?

Just as all of Scripture points to the cross of Jesus and the identification of Him as God's Son and the coming Messiah, we too can find and embrace a new identity when we immerse ourselves in God's Word. When we read the Bible with the expectation of finding Jesus, we'll begin to see that through faith in Him and His works we are adopted into God's family as His children and are given new identities. Sadly, we often forget this truth and have to be reminded of it daily. If we're not memorizing and meditating on God's Word on a consistent basis, we cannot expect to fend off Satan's attacks. The more we study God's Word, the more we learn about this our identities and what God expects from us as His children.

The more we study God's Word, the more we learn about our new identities and what God expects from us as His children.

What are some challenges believers face when they read the Bible? Discuss some ways they can overcome these challenges?

ENGAGE

Charles Spurgeon, a well-known preacher from the 19th century, once said: "As the rain soaks into the ground, so pray the Lord to let His gospel soak into your soul."[2] It is the repetitive pounding of the moisture into the earth that transforms it from a parched, dusty, hard ground to rich, moist, useful soil. When God's Word saturates into our thirsty souls, we will experience transformation.

Perhaps a better metaphor would be one that happens in the kitchen. Consider how meat is often saturated (sometimes for hours) in a marinade so that it will be more tender and flavorful. With that imagery in mind, consider what it would be like to saturate your entire life in God's Word in such a way that it transforms you from ordinary to extraordinary, much like a piece of meat gets completely transformed after it has been saturated in a great marinade.

In your last few minutes together, spend some time discussing ways that someone's life can be transformed by immersing himself or herself in Scripture. If there are specific passages or personal stories that come to mind be sure to share those with the group. This exercise will help you see the variety of ways in which the Bible speaks and hopefully inspires believers to delve more fully into His Word.

PRAYER REQUESTS

....

....

....

....

....

....

....

....

....

....

....

....

1. John Calvin, *The Gospel According to John 1–10* (Grand Rapids: Wm. B. Eerdmans Publishing, Co., 1961), 139.
2. Charles Spurgeon, as quoted at *spurgeononline.com*. Accessed April 29, 2015.

In addition to studying God's Word, work with your group leader to create a plan for personal study, worship, and application between now and the next session. Select from the following optional activities to match your personal preferences and available time.

⬆ Worship

☑ Read your Bible. Complete the reading plan on page 16.

☐ Spend time with God by engaging the devotional experience on page 17.

➡ ⬅ Personal Study

☐ Read and interact with "Marinade Instructions" on page 18.

☐ Read and interact with "The Transforming Power of Scripture" on page 20.

⬅ ➡ Application

☐ Memorize Hebrews 4:12: "For the word of God is living and effective and sharper than any double-edged sword, penetrating as far as the separation of soul and spirit, joints and marrow. It is able to judge the ideas and thoughts of the heart."

☐ Spend time journaling. Just as Jesus countered each of Satan's temptations by quoting Scripture, Jesus often turned to God's Word as the authority for His life. Journal about a time when God's Word spoke to you and you did something differently as a result. What happened? How did it impact your perception of Scripture?

☐ Share with others. Take time to contact a few people this week with encouragements from Scripture. This could be people within your group or those outside your group that you sense need an encouraging word.

☐ Other:

 **WORSHIP**

READING PLAN

Read through the following Scripture passages this week. Use the space provided to record your thoughts and responses.

Day 1
2 Timothy 3:10-17

Day 2
Psalm 19:1-14

Day 3
Joshua 1:1-9

Day 4
1 Corinthians 15:1-11

Day 5
Psalm 119:89-112

Day 6
1 Peter 1:13-25

Day 7
Deuteronomy 6:1-9

IMMERSE YOURSELF IN GOD'S WORD

Perhaps you are wondering: *How do I immerse myself in God's Word? What does that look like day-to-day?* This week find a verse that you want to soak in and get to know. If you don't have one on the top of your mind, use one from the daily reading plan on the previous page. Follow the steps below and answer all the questions before your group meets again.

Your passage: _____

Memorize and Know Scripture

Write this passage from memory below.

How would you explain this passage in your own words?

Meditate and Believe Scripture

What does this passage say is true about God?

What does this passage say is true about you?

Exercise and Apply Scripture

How are you believing or not believing in the truth of this passage?

How can you show someone else the truth of this passage?

MARINADE INSTRUCTIONS

For marinade, or God's Word, to completely saturate something, or someone, there are four things that need to happen. We need to get in, get under, get through, and get transformed.

Get In: Just like an item needs to get into the marinade and be completely soaked, we've got to get into Scripture. First, once we begin a relationship with Jesus, we receive God's Spirit who enables us to understand Scripture in a way we never could before (see 1 Cor. 2:14-15). Second, when we grasp that the story of God revealed in Scripture spans from eternity past to eternity future, we begin to understand that our lives are actually a storyline within God's Story. We find the context for who we are as we begin to let God narrate and shape our existence through His Word. Finally, over time, we will actually begin to get into Scripture like we do a great book or movie. We actually look forward to it. We desire it!

> *Have you ever thought about your life being a storyline within God's story? How does that make you feel?*

> *What are typically the biggest distractions from you getting in the Word and allowing God to be the narrator of your life?*

Every story about God's people throughout Scripture is a story about your spiritual family tree. If you are a Christian you have been adopted into God's family. Their story is yours. Every label that has been given to God's people has been given to you. Through faith in Jesus, this is just a partial list of who you are:

- God's child (Gal. 3:26)
- Part of "a chosen [people], a royal priesthood, a holy nation," and a treasured possession (1 Pet. 2:9)
- A "new creation" (2 Cor. 5:17)
- A member of "the body of Christ" (1 Cor. 12:27)
- God's friend (John 15:15)
- A citizen of heaven (Phil. 3:20)
- An ambassador for Christ (2 Cor. 5:20).

Get Under: Just like an item benefits from being completely under the marinade, we need to get under Scripture. It's been said that we can't understand Scripture until we stand under it. This means that the posture of our hearts can't "stand above" Scripture, picking and choosing what we like and don't like as we read it. Rather, we must "stand under" Scripture and allow the posture of our hearts to be open to God's Word to have authority over us. Much more than just reading Scripture, we must let Scripture read us (see Heb. 4:12).

Take a step back and think about how you approach Scripture. When are you most likely to "stand above" Scripture as described here?

When we stand above Scripture and the posture of our hearts has more authority in our lives than God's Word, it is tempting to believe partial truths or even lies about ourselves rather than the truest things that God says about us.

Get Through: Just like the marinade over time begins to work its way through the item being marinated, we need to let Scripture get through us. Often, people focus on getting through a specific length of Scripture at a time or over the course of a season. For example, while it is wonderful to get through the entire Bible in a year, you may experience a greater impact when you focus more on one passage or biblical truth at a time. Sometimes we need to read and let in the same passage of Scripture for weeks before it really begins to get through and change us.

Let the truth of God's Word get through every layer of who you are. Let it soak into your heart, your mind, and your memories. Re-examine the list of verses on the previous page and pray that God would allow you to trust in this identity for yourself. Take hope in the truth that if you are in Christ, God has given you a new story, a new narrative, that describes you.

Which identifying mark from the list do you find most difficult to believe?

Get Transformed: Just like marinade tenderizes and transforms anything that soaks in it for a long time, God's Word transforms any person who immerses his or her entire life in it. The exponentially beautiful truth of Scripture is that, unlike mere marinade that eventually reaches its limit in transforming an item, there is no limit to the transforming power of God's Word in our lives. We could spend every minute of the rest of our lives soaking in Scripture and we would continue to be transformed through God's Spirit into the image of Jesus more and more.

How have you seen the transforming power of Scripture, either in your life or in the life of someone you know?

THE TRANSFORMING POWER OF SCRIPTURE

As anybody who has ever marinated a piece of chicken, fish, steak, or vegetable knows, it's not enough to just have marinade sitting on the shelf in the same room as the item. The same is true for a Bible that merely sits on a shelf. In fact, it's not enough to simply open up the bottle of marinade. The same is also true for simply opening up the Bible and expecting deep transformation.

Jesus was saturated in the truth of God's Word clearly and continually. He knew who He was and the life God designed and desired for Him to live. He experienced every moment of His life knowing God and being known by Him. As a follower of Jesus, it's essential that we too immerse ourselves in God's Word so that our entire lives can be transformed into the truest lives that God has for us.

Let's take a closer look at a passage we studied in the group time:

> 12 The word of God is living and effective and sharper than any double-edged sword, penetrating as far as the separation of soul and spirit, joints and marrow. It is able to judge the ideas and thoughts of the heart. 13 No creature is hidden from Him, but all things are naked and exposed to the eyes of Him to whom we must give an account.
> **HEBREWS 4:12-13**

Is there an area of your life that currently needs the penetrating and transforming power of God's Word?

What does verse 12 mean when it says God's Word is "living and effective"?

The word *sword* in verse 12 requires some additional attention. This metaphor suggests that the Bible functions much like a surgeon's scalpel when a doctor carefully identifies the location for the incision, penetrates the flesh with the depth that's required, and with great accuracy cuts out the infected area. Similarly, and with the Spirit's guidance, God's Word is a tool that clears away the infected parts of our hearts, transforming us to look more like His Son.

Is this a helpful metaphor? How have you experienced Scripture locating infected areas of your heart?

There are millions of books in print today that are being read throughout the world. Most of us only have the time to read just a few of those each year—and only some of those ever have any kind of meaningful impact on our lives.

The Bible is different. It's on another level than all the other books we can get in our hands. Why? Because it's the very Word of God that tell us about Himself and guides us through life. It's living and active. We don't read it so much as we experience its transforming power.

> 105 Your word is a lamp for my feet
> and a light on my path.
> 106 I have solemnly sworn
> to keep Your righteous judgments.
> 107 I am severely afflicted;
> LORD, give me life through Your word.
> 108 LORD, please accept my willing offerings of praise,
> and teach me Your judgments.
> 109 My life is constantly in danger,
> yet I do not forget Your instruction.
> 110 The wicked have set a trap for me,
> but I have not wandered from Your precepts.
> 111 I have Your decrees as a heritage forever;
> indeed, they are the joy of my heart.
> 112 I am resolved to obey Your statutes
> to the very end.
> **PSALM 119:105-112**

How does this passage describe a life that's dependent upon God's Word?

How would it change your relationship with God if you allowed Him to narrate your life using the words of Scripture?

CONNECTED THROUGH PRAYER

Prayer is our response to God's constant
invitation to interact with Him.

REFLECT

We examined in the first session how by immersing ourselves in God's Word we will both discover our identities and build a foundation for transformation to take place in our lives. We learned that the Bible tells us who God is, who we are, and why we exist. And while it's important to read the Bible, *how* we read it may be even more important. Ultimately, being saturated in God's Holy Word will transform how we see God, ourselves, our lives, and the world around us.

Which of the assignments did you explore this week? How did it go?

What did you learn or experience while reading the Bible?

What questions would you like to ask?

PRAY

Begin the session by connecting with God through prayer. Use the following guidelines as you speak with Him:

- Acknowledge that God alone is worthy of worship, honor, praise, and adoration.

- Thank the all-knowing, all-powerful, perfect God for inviting imperfect people like us to interact with Him.

- Acknowledge that there are so many things pulling our attention away from Him. Ask that God would remove all distractions for this time of study.

- Thank God for being the true source of every good and perfect gift in our lives.

INTRODUCTION

It has been said that there is only one person in the kingdom who can wake up the king at midnight to ask for a glass of water without fear of being punished—the king's kid. Through faith in Jesus, we are the King's kid. Yet we often forget that we have been invited to have limitless interactions with an infinite God. Whether it is because we take it for granted or we allow ourselves to be wrapped up in earthly things, we often neglect and fail to enjoy this tremendous gift of prayer.

As we take a closer look at Jesus' life, it quickly becomes apparent that Jesus consistently responded to God the Father's invitation to interact with Him. Whether Jesus was alone or with others, He was constantly aware of the Father and engaged in continual conversations with Him. Time with God was a critical high priority in Jesus' life.

In the same way that Jesus interacted with God, so too can we. Prayer is far more than a one-way monologue, listing our wishes before God. Instead, prayer can be as dynamic, intimate, and engaging as the way we interact with those closest to us. Prayer involves waiting, listening, remembering, affirming, pleading, petitioning, thanking, confessing, worshiping, and so much more.

To get off on the right foot, we must remember a foundational aspect of prayer: Prayer doesn't actually begin with us; it begins with God. God has already initiated an interaction with us through a variety of ways and means but most fully through His Son, Jesus. Through faith in Christ, we have become the beloved child of the King, who is always welcoming us into His presence. Because prayer is a continuous response to God's interaction, we can have confidence that God hears, knows, and is present to our interactions with Him. Though it may feel like we're the ones initiating the conversation and God is silent, the truth is God is always waiting and inviting us to engage with Him. He is ready, willing, and able to listen, not just to our words but also to our hearts.

Discuss for a moment the ways in which we interact with those closest to us.

Does the description of prayer—our response to God's constant invitation to interact with Him—differ from your perspective of it? If so, how?

KNOW THE STORY

Though you can find numerous examples of Jesus interacting with God throughout the Bible, probably the most famous prayer in all of Scripture is the prayer that Jesus taught His disciples. This is the centerpiece amid the set of foundational teachings on a variety of topics addressed by Christ, commonly referred to as the Sermon on the Mount.

5 Whenever you pray, you must not be like the hypocrites, because they love to pray standing in the synagogues and on the street corners to be seen by people. I assure you: They've got their reward! 6 But when you pray, go into your private room, shut your door, and pray to your Father who is in secret. And your Father who sees in secret will reward you. 7 When you pray, don't babble like the idolaters, since they imagine they'll be heard for their many words. 8 Don't be like them, because your Father knows the things you need before you ask Him.

9 Therefore, you should pray like this:
　　Our Father in heaven,
　　Your name be honored as holy.
　　10 Your kingdom come.
　　Your will be done
　　on earth as it is in heaven.
　　11 Give us today our daily bread.
　　12 And forgive us our debts,
　　as we also have forgiven our debtors.
　　13 And do not bring us into temptation,
　　but deliver us from the evil one.
　　For Yours is the kingdom and the power
　　and the glory forever. Amen.
MATTHEW 6:5-13

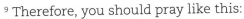

Discuss the differences you see between verses 5-8 and 9-13.

When you read this prayer, what is mentioned that resonates most with what you need from God right now?

UNPACK THE STORY

A MODEL FOR PRAYER

Before teaching the disciples this framework for prayer, Jesus first tells them two ways *not* to pray. Jesus first warns them against being like the hypocrites who pray for show. He then warns them against being like the pagans who babble empty words. What is wrong with both of these approaches to prayer? Neither is interested in relating and engaging with the one true living God. The first group is uttering words with pomp and circumstance in highly visible public areas like the temple or street corners so that people will see their religious activity and think highly of them. The second group of people from other religions is uttering a high volume of magical, formulaic words, while hoping in vain that their false gods will respond. Jesus reminds His disciples that God sees everything, already knows what they need, and wants to be in close relationship as a father to a child.

How could one's prayer life be transformed if he or she started praying knowing that God sees everything and already knows what we need?

How could one's prayer life be transformed if he or she recognized that the purpose of prayer is to bring us into a closer relationship with God?

Jesus is reminding His listeners and us that prayer isn't the means to get what we want; it's the means to draw near to God and get to know Him better.

The distinguishing characteristic between the groups Jesus warns against and the people Jesus wants us to be is the motivation and means behind why they do what they do. The two groups above pray to use God and people to get closer to things they want. Jesus, however, urges the disciples to be people who pray to get close to the living God.

In this context, Jesus is reminding His listeners and us that prayer isn't the means to get what we want; it's the means to draw near to God and get to know Him better. God is our focus! With that as our primary motivation, the content of the Lord's Prayer then models for us how we can interact with God in a way that draws us closer to Him. Out of the overflow of our response to God's invitation to limitless interaction with Him, we can experience more of the life that God designed and desires for us.

A FRAMEWORK FOR PRAYER

We find six key elements to incorporate into our prayer lives, whether in private or in public, as we delve deeper into the Lord's Prayer as a framework for how we can interact with God.

1. Remembering—"Our Father in heaven"
2. Adoring—"Your name be honored as holy."
3. Inviting—"Your Kingdom come … on earth as it is in heaven."
4. Requesting—"Give us today our daily bread."
5. Confessing/Releasing—"Forgive us our debts, as we also have forgiven our debtors."
6. Petitioning—"Do not bring us into temptation, but deliver us from the evil one."

Using the Lord's Prayer as a framework is a fantastic way to assess your prayer life. Take a few moments to discuss these elements with your group in regard to your own prayer life.

Which of the six elements of the Lord's Prayer do you think will be most natural for you? Which one will be least intuitive for you?

What are ways you can grow in incorporating a specific element into your interactions with God?

Prayer is both the easiest thing and the hardest thing we can do. It is easy in that God constantly invites us to connect with Him through prayer anywhere and anytime. Yet, it is also quite difficult because it requires dependence on God, faith that He loves us, trust that He will show up, and conviction that He will respond and communicate with us. Prayer also requires some hard work on our part—we need to show up regularly and be available, authentic, and vulnerable, so that we can hear whatever God has for us.

Which aspect of prayer have you experienced most recently?

Prayer also requires some hard work on our part—we need to show up regularly and be available, authentic, and vulnerable so that we can hear whatever God has for us.

ENGAGE

Praying together was a frequent practice for the early church. Acts 4:23-31 gives us an example of an actual prayer that Peter and John prayed with other believers. Read and discuss this passage together.

[23] After they were released, they went to their own people and reported everything the chief priests and the elders had said to them. [24] When they heard this, they all raised their voices to God and said, "Master, You are the One who made the heaven, the earth, and the sea, and everything in them. [25] You said through the Holy Spirit, by the mouth of our father David Your servant:

> Why did the Gentiles rage
> and the peoples plot futile things?
> [26] The kings of the earth took their stand
> and the rulers assembled together
> against the Lord and against His Messiah.

[27] "For, in fact, in this city both Herod and Pontius Pilate, with the Gentiles and the people of Israel, assembled together against Your holy Servant Jesus, whom You anointed, [28] to do whatever Your hand and Your plan had predestined to take place. [29] And now, Lord, consider their threats, and grant that Your slaves may speak Your message with complete boldness, [30] while You stretch out Your hand for healing, signs, and wonders to be performed through the name of Your holy Servant Jesus." [31] When they had prayed, the place where they were assembled was shaken, and they were all filled with the Holy Spirit and began to speak God's message with boldness.
ACTS 4:23-31

How would you describe the sincerity and passion with which this prayer is voiced?

How is this prayer similar to or different from the typical way you or your group prays?

As you take prayer requests and close in prayer, intentionally incorporate some of the same sincerity and passion from this passage.

In addition to studying God's Word, work with your group leader to create a plan for personal study, worship, and application between now and the next session. Select from the following optional activities to match your personal preferences and available time.

⬆ Worship

☑ Read your Bible. Complete the reading plan on page 30.

☐ Spend time with God by engaging the devotional experience on page 31.

☐ Connect with God each day by taking a "prayer walk" around your neighborhood. As you walk past homes and buildings, pray for the people who live or work there. Ask God to move their hearts toward Christ if they do not know Him yet, or if they do, pray for their love for Jesus to be deepened and their lives to reflect Him well.

➡ ⬅ Personal Study

☐ Read and interact with "A Model for Prayer" on page 32.

☐ Read and interact with "A Framework for Prayer" on page 34.

⬅ ➡ Application

☐ Most of Jesus' prayers were not for Himself but for others. This type of intercessory prayer is a wonderful way to care for others and helps us develop more compassionate hearts for them. Pray for someone else in need today, perhaps even for someone who is difficult for you to love. See how God changes your perspective about that person as you pray for him or her over time.

☐ Pray through Psalm 23 this week. Pray through it one line at a time. For example, read verse 1: "The LORD is my shepherd; there is nothing I lack." Then personalize it saying, "Thank You, God, for being the Good Shepherd, the One who loves me and takes good care of me, meeting all of my needs." Continue until you pray through all of the verses.

☐ Memorize Ephesians 6:18: "Pray at all times in the Spirit with every prayer and request, and stay alert in this with all perseverance and intercession for all the saints."

☐ Other:

 **WORSHIP**

READING PLAN

Read through the following Scripture passages this week. Use the space provided to record your thoughts and responses.

Day 1
Luke 11:1-13

Day 2
Philippians 4:4-7

Day 3
1 Timothy 2:1-7

Day 4
Ephesians 6:10-20

Day 5
James 5:13-18

Day 6
1 Thessalonians 5:16-22

Day 7
Hebrews 4:11-16

MAKE IT PERSONAL

Spend some time during this devotion meditating on and journaling through the Lord's Prayer. Read Matthew 6:9-13 one more time and familiarize yourself with the "A Framework for Prayer" on page 27. Follow its example by personalizing and writing down words that come to mind, Scripture passages that relate, and/or how you've experienced God in relation to each of the elements below:

REMEMBER:

ADORE:

INVITE:

REQUEST:

CONFESS/RELEASE:

PETITION:

A MODEL FOR PRAYER

Throughout the Gospels, God has given us Jesus as a model for prayer. Scripture shows us who Jesus prayed for, when He prayed, where He prayed, how He prayed, and why He prayed. We would be wise to look to Him as we attempt to strengthen our prayer lives.

So when and where did Jesus pray? The short answer is everywhere and anywhere. In fact, Jesus' prayers never appeared to be repetitive formulas but rather were filled with life, emotion, and rich language that evidenced Jesus' dynamic, deep, constant, and mutually interactive relationship with God the Father. Consider the variety of Jesus' interactions with God that model an anytime-and-everywhere type of prayer life for us.

We have also been invited to experience limitless interaction with God everywhere at anytime. We can interact with God while driving, cleaning, working, playing, laying down, sitting up, running, and so forth. In fact, there is no place or no time in which we cannot interact with God.

> *Where and when is the most natural place and time for you to interact with God regularly through prayer?*

> *When and where do you have the opportunity to interact with God that you are not currently doing so?*

Jesus began His ministry praying and ended His ministry praying from the cross. Jesus prayed in the morning, during the day, and at night. Jesus prayed in the mountains, the wilderness, the garden, and the city. It's no wonder that we've been instructed to pray constantly and everywhere.

Jesus prayed short prayers that spanned just a sentence and long prayers that spanned the entire night. No matter how short or long Jesus interacted with God, He taught us that we should never be repetitious, mistakenly thinking that the more words we use the more God will hear us. Like a relationship with the closest people in our lives, sometimes a few words are all that are needed to communicate the depths of our hearts. Other times, hours in conversation seem to pass by without labor because of the rich, enjoyable connection.

When Jesus prayed, sometimes He made requests of God. He prayed for His needs, His disciples' needs, and our needs. Jesus modeled this for us even though He taught that God already knows our needs before we ask Him. Jesus prayed for those who loved Him and those who rejected Him. Jesus gave thanks to God in His prayers for food, gave thanks for God's nature, and gave thanks that God heard His prayers.

Amid all the requests, prayers for others, and thanksgiving, Jesus trusted God obediently, even in the midst of tremendous anguish. There's no greater evidence of this than Jesus' agony in the garden of Gethsemane where He asked that God would take the cup of suffering away from Him and yet prayed, "nevertheless, not My will, but Yours, be done" (Luke 22:42).

Though Jesus taught against praying in public just to be seen by others, Jesus prayed in public for the good of others, teaching us that even in public prayer our focus is on God rather than those around us. But even though Jesus prayed in public, as we follow the biblical record of His prayer life, we'll also notice a recurring phrase, "Jesus withdrew." While it would be an accurate observation that Jesus prayed in both public and private, there seems to be a significance to His private prayers—prayers that none of the Gospel writers were able to record because Jesus prayed them after coming apart from the crowd and those closest to Himself.

How does the variety and scope of Jesus' interactions with God through prayer encourage you?

How does Jesus as a model for prayer challenge your current patterns of prayer?

In a world where we can be bombarded with a constant stream of external stimulation, there is a need more than ever to follow Jesus' example of withdrawing into quiet places to cultivate a relationship with God through prayer. The more often we do this, the more quickly we can free ourselves from the burdens and distractions that seek to ensnare us, and the more we will become like Jesus.

A FRAMEWORK FOR PRAYER

Let's be reminded of and dive deeper into the framework of prayer provided for us in the Lord's Prayer. Consider these elements we find in Matthew 6:9-13 as action steps to implement into your prayer life.

> [9] "Therefore, you should pray like this:
> Our Father in heaven,
> Your name be honored as holy.
> [10] Your kingdom come.
> Your will be done
> on earth as it is in heaven.
> [11] Give us today our daily bread.
> [12] And forgive us our debts,
> as we also have forgiven our debtors.
> [13] And do not bring us into temptation,
> but deliver us from the evil one.
> For Yours is the kingdom and the power
> and the glory forever. Amen.
> **MATTHEW 6:9-13**

Remembering—"Our Father in heaven": We begin our interaction with God acknowledging who He has revealed Himself to be. He is our Father, Creator, Sustainer, Provider, Protector, and so much more. He is all-powerful, all-knowing, and all-sufficient. As we immerse our lives in God's Word, we can learn more about who God has revealed Himself to be.

Adoring—"Your name be honored as holy": We continue our interaction with God acknowledging that His character and His reputation are worthy of our fully-surrendered worship. We remember God's faithfulness throughout Scripture and in our lives. We acknowledge and affirm that God is who God says He is, and we respond in worship. We value God's truth and His direction over the opinion of others.

Inviting—"Your kingdom come ... on earth as it is in heaven": We invite God's reign and rule which is perfect in heaven to be present in our lives and in our world. We submit to God's ways as being superior to our ways.

Requesting—"Give us today our daily bread": We ask for today's needs. We don't worry about tomorrow or get ahead of ourselves planning. We share the concerns we have for ourselves and others even as we acknowledge God's sovereignty and power change people and situations according to His perfect will. We freely ask for what we want, while trusting that God in His grace and love will provide what is best for us.

Confessing/Releasing—"Forgive us our debts, as we also have forgiven our debtors": We embrace our forgiveness through Jesus' power over sin in our lives even as we extend forgiveness through Jesus' power over those who have hurt us. We release our feelings of shame to God, our pain from others, and our need to condemn others.

Petitioning—"Do not bring us into temptation, but deliver us from the evil one": We ask for God's leading moving forward, a renewed focus on His design and desire for us, and protection from anything that distracts us from life with Him.

Learn from this framework of prayer and incorporate it into your prayer life. Be intentional about interacting with God in each of the areas of remembering, adoring, inviting, requesting, confessing, releasing, and petitioning.

> *Which one of these elements do you have the most difficulty with? Why do you think it is so difficult?*

> *Scripture refers to Jesus withdrawing Himself from potential distractions to pray. Identify a place and a time of day that you can withdraw to spend uninterrupted and focused time in order to interact with God.*

SESSION 3

LIVING IN COMMUNITY

We are called to live authentically
and interdependently with one
another in biblical community

REFLECT

As we learned in the previous session, prayer is an invitation to interact with our Creator. Prayer isn't a presentation of our wish list to God. It involves waiting, listening, remembering, affirming, pleading, petitioning, thanking, confessing, worshiping, and so much more. God is ready, willing, and able to listen not just to our words but also our hearts. Because of Christ, we have become children of the Father, who is always welcoming us into His presence.

Which of the assignments did you explore this week? How did it go?

What did you learn or experience while reading the Bible?

What questions would you like to ask?

PRAY

Begin the session by connecting with God through prayer. Use the following guidelines as you speak with Him:

- Ask God to show us how we have been created for community and the ways in which we can cultivate community as disciples of Jesus.

- Thank God for your church family with whom you worship, pray, and serve, for how He has used other believers to help you grow, and for the group of people you are with at this moment.

- Acknowledge and praise God that the brothers and sisters who share your faith and commitment to following Jesus are a gift from God to encourage you in the ups and downs of life.

- Ask the Holy Spirit to intervene in this time of study that you may build more authentic relationships that move you forward in loving God and loving others.

INTRODUCTION

Beyond the city limits of San Francisco exists a land of giants. Redwood trees so tall that if they were to lay down on a football-field-length bed their feet would hang off the edge another 10 feet. Tree trunks so wide that a school bus could hide behind and you'd never see it. In the Armstrong Redwoods National State Reserve, there is even a tree that is estimated to have stood tall for more than 1,400 years.

While so many are amazed by these ancient trees as they extend skyward toward the heavens, what is even more awe-inspiring is how they have extended underground. It is the root system of these ancient redwood trees that has enabled them to stand strong against threatening winds and violent storms that could rip them from their foundation. Yet, their roots do not extend vertically deep into the ground. Surprisingly, redwood tree roots typically go no more than 12 feet below ground, hardly enough to sustain 300-feet-tall trees through the centuries of destructive weather. So, how is it possible that redwoods have survived in this area, enabling countless people to stand in wonder with eyes toward the heavens to take in the immensity of these creatures, the tallest living things on this planet? The answer can be summed up in one word—*community.*

Amazingly, these ancient redwoods have underground roots that extend outwards of 150 feet, interlocking with the root systems of other redwoods in the grove. Beneath the feet of visiting onlookers, these giants hold one another up in a community of inter-woven roots. Because of this, their stability and strength is multiplied as their foundation becomes larger than their height. They have been able to grow large and strong because they have done it together.

What are some words or emotions that come to mind when you picture an ancient redwood grove with a vast root system that is interwoven and interdependent upon each other?

How does the metaphor of the redwoods describe the church?

The only way we can endure the storms of life and thrive as God intended us to is through our fellow believers. Our spiritual roots must extend, not just deep but wide, spread among the lives of those around us. Just as there is no redwood tree that has endured for centuries without the help of other redwood trees, there is no such thing as a disciple who thrives without the community of other disciples.

KNOW THE STORY

The first followers of Jesus were some of the most diverse people you could imagine. There were zealots (like Simon) who came from a radicalized political party that were known for assassinating government officials (like Matthew, a tax collector). There were former pagans who enjoyed eating food that any Jewish person would not only find repulsive but against Mosaic Law. There were misfits, social pariahs, men, women, children, singles, marrieds, widows, orphans, type A's, cynics, and those with low self-esteem. Yet, this diverse community was remarkably unified around one thing: Jesus.

The Book of Acts chronicles the 30 years of the early church's explosion beyond social, geographic, ethnic, and religious boundaries through the power of the Holy Spirit. The author, Luke, records with much detail, giving us many moving pictures of the type of community that can be cultivated amid tremendous diversity and adversity. They were often violently persecuted and yet they were as committed to one another as they were committed to their Savior. Rather than using the community to build up their individual resources and agendas, individuals in the early church used their resources to build up the community of believers.

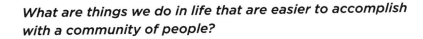

What are things we do in life that are easier to accomplish with a community of people?

Briefly discuss the similarities and differences between your relationships with other believers and with non-believers.

One of the foundational descriptions of the early church is found in Acts 2, where Luke writes,

> [42] And they devoted themselves to the apostles' teaching, to the fellowship, to the breaking of bread, and to the prayers. [43] Then fear came over everyone, and many wonders and signs were being performed through the apostles. [44] Now all the believers were together and held all things in common. [45] They sold their possessions and property and distributed the proceeds to all, as anyone had a need. [46] Every day they devoted themselves to meeting together in the temple complex, and broke bread from house to house. They ate their food with a joyful and humble attitude, [47] praising God and having favor with all the people. And every day the Lord added to them those who were being saved.
> **ACTS 2:42-47**

UNPACK THE STORY

EXPERIENCING LIFE TOGETHER

The richness of the Greek language must also be noted to grasp the depth of community this diverse group of people experienced. In Acts 2, we find the word "together" mentioned twice in our English translation. However, two different Greek words are used in each of these instances and once understood, you'll never think of "together" the same way again.

The first Greek word is *epi*. It's a word that is used to describe the physical location of something. Luke basically is telling us that the first followers of Jesus were in close proximity to one another. They didn't see each other twice a month; rather the first followers of Jesus frequently rubbed shoulders with one another, ate, prayed, worshiped, and experienced the richness of life together.

> The first followers of Jesus frequently rubbed shoulders with one another, ate, prayed, worshiped, and experienced the richness of life together.

However, just having proximity with one another doesn't lead to deep, authentic, biblical community. Perhaps this is why Luke uses a different Greek word later in Acts 2 to describe this group of people living in proximity with one another. The second Greek word is *homothumadon,* and it's a word on an entirely different level than *epi*. Its meaning transcends physical space and is a togetherness that occurs on a deeper spiritual and emotional level. It's only found 12 times in the New Testament, and Luke uses the word 11 times in Acts.

What about this Acts 2 description of biblical community is appealing? What about it is terrifying?

Why do you think many people find it difficult to be meaningfully devoted to a group of believers?

Knit together by the Holy Spirit dwelling within them and hearts ablaze and fixed on Jesus, their world (and the world) was turned upside down because of the depth of their community.

COMMUNITY VS. PROXIMITY

On our discipleship journey, it's common to mistake proximity for community. It's easy to think that "being around" other followers of Jesus is what it means to be in community. However, proximity and community are two distinctive things that result in two different outcomes.

In the same way that redwood tree root systems offer us an apt metaphor for community, tree nurseries offer us a vivid picture of proximity. Tree nurseries, like the natural environment for redwoods, are filled with many trees. In tree nurseries, the trees are growing and are healthy. From a distance, the trees in a tree nursery appear to be in community with one another. They are closely situated, and in some cases, their branches are even touching one another.

However, when a strong storm rips through a tree nursery, many trees are toppled over, unable to stand like the redwoods. The difference is that the trees in a nursery have never truly been in community, they have only been in proximity. Each tree in a nursery exists within its own planter box. The trees in tree nurseries grow, but only in isolation. Their roots extend, yet they are never able to get the stability that redwoods have because they are not interconnected or interdependent. True, some of the trees in the nursery don't topple over, giving the illusion of stability. However, it's likely that the trees still standing are located on the interior of the nursery while the trees on the fringes of the nursery have taken the fall.

Why is proximity a necessary but shallow substitute for community?

Why do our groups and our churches so often settle for mere proximity rather than pursue true biblical community?

If you cultivate community, you always get proximity.

Much of what we call community in our church today is simply proximity. Standing next to one another in a worship service, serving alongside one another on a project, even sitting on a couch with the same people week after week doesn't necessarily mean that community is being cultivated. If you settle for proximity, you rarely get deep community. However, if you cultivate community, you always get proximity.

ENGAGE

Scripture is flooded with what has been referred to as "one another" verses—100 times in the New Testament to be exact. These verses help us go beyond proximity and begin to cultivate deep, authentic, biblical community. These verses are not just suggestions or recommendations from Scripture, but in many cases, they are framed in the imperative, as commands to be obeyed.

Several of these "one another" verses call us to encourage one another. This is a key aspect of life together in biblical community. To practice this in a concrete way, prepare index cards that have the name of each person in the group on individual cards. Ask everyone to write an encouraging note for each person in the group. This could be something they appreciate about the person or how they have seen God work in that person. If they don't know the person it could be framed as a prayer that God would use this person in a significant way. Once you have finished with one card, pass the card to the right and continue with the next card. Eventually the card will return to the person whose name is on it. This is a powerful way to affirm each person and the ways in which God is working in them.

What are your observations from this activity?

What are some things that would happen to a biblical community if encouragement and affirmation were common practice?

PRAYER REQUESTS

....

....

....

....

....

....

....

....

....

In addition to studying God's Word, work with your group leader to create a plan for personal study, worship, and application between now and the next session. Select from the following optional activities to match your personal preferences and available time.

↑ Worship

☑ Read your Bible. Complete the reading plan on page 44.

☐ Spend time with God by engaging the devotional experience on page 45.

☐ Connect with God each day through prayer. Pick one or two characteristics of the Acts 2 church that you aren't currently experiencing. Pray that God would reveal action plans for you to incorporate into your community. Take time to listen to all God has to say.

➡ ⬅ Personal Study

☐ Read and interact with "Experiencing Life Together" on page 46.

☐ Read and interact with "One Anothers" on page 48.

⬅ ➡ Application

☐ God often uses people to change people. Journal about a time when God used another person or a group of believers to encourage or challenge you to move toward Jesus and His way of life. Likewise, share a time when you were used by God to encourage or challenge someone else.

☐ Connect with someone from your group this week. Make an appointment to meet for coffee or lunch. When you meet, ask each other two questions: (1) How has God been working in you and your life lately? and (2) How can I pray for you? Then plan to follow up in the coming weeks.

☐ Memorize John 13:34-35: "I give you a new command: Love one another. Just as I have loved you, you must also love one another. By this all people will know that you are My disciples, if you have love for one another."

☐ Other:

WORSHIP

READING PLAN

Read through the following Scripture passages this week. Use the space provided to record your thoughts and responses.

Day 1
Romans 12:3-13

Day 2
Philippians 2:1-13

Day 3
Hebrews 10:19-25

Day 4
Ecclesiastes 4:1-16

Day 5
1 Peter 4:7-11

Day 6
1 Corinthians 12:12-31

Day 7
John 15:12-17

TOGETHER

The believers we see in Acts 2 weren't just an affinity group that got together on a semi-regular basis and enjoyed an activity together. They experienced life together. There were no isolated "lone ranger Christians." Far from it. They immersed their lives in God's Word together, prayed together, shared each other's burdens, laughed together, cried together, parented together, ate together, celebrated the Lord's Supper together, lived with thanksgiving together, served together, gave sacrificially together, and were daily hospitable to newcomers together.

Every member of this Acts 2 group knew each other and they were known by one another. They belonged. They were embraced. They were challenged. They experienced conflict and reconciliation. They forgave and were forgiven. They loved and were loved. This small, ever-growing group was able to change the world because they focused on God's mission together.

Make two lists of deeds and activities the early Christians did together that you are currently experiencing with other believers and that you would like to experience with other believers.

Already Doing

Not Yet Doing

What are some of the barriers to true fellowship or authentic "life-on-life" relationships in our culture today? What are some cultural values we hold that hinder our interdependence upon one another?

EXPERIENCING LIFE TOGETHER

Let's look closer at the second meaning for the English word "together" we find in Acts 2: *Homothumadon*. Perhaps you have experienced glimpses of *homothumadon*. If you've ever been part of a large crowd at a concert and everyone in attendance is singing along to that song everyone has been waiting for, that is *homothumadon*. Or if you've been to a sporting event and tens of thousands of fans erupt into celebration when their team scores the game winner—that's a taste of *homothumadon* as we see it in Acts 2. It's literally a mob mentality where the many become one, caught up in something greater and bigger than themselves.

Homothumadon is a combination of words that literally mean "the same fiery passion." Some English versions use the tame translation, "one accord," but *homothumadon* has the intensity of a unified crowd. And when used to describe the early church, it was the most beautiful riot ever witnessed. It was a riot of belonging, service, love, patience, hospitality, inclusiveness, and so much more. Yes, the early church was in physical proximity together, but they were also dynamically and spiritually together.

Take some time to describe your best experience with a small community of believers. What are the elements that made that community supportive and memorable?

How did God use the people in that community to impact your life?

As this *epi-* and *homothumadon*-rich community swelled in size, even passionate enemies of the early church were transformed and brought into the very community they once hated. Though there were many examples throughout history, perhaps one of the most famous is found in Scripture—the self-righteous Saul who became the Christ-focused Paul after encountering the resurrected Jesus on a road. As Paul began experiencing the transforming effects of a Christ-centered community, and as he grew in his faith, he became one of the greatest champions of biblical community.

In one of his letters to the community of Christians in Corinth, Paul borrowed the metaphor of the human body to instruct his readers on how much they need one another in community.

 PERSONAL STUDY

¹² For as the body is one and has many parts, and all the parts of that body, though many, are one body—so also is Christ. ¹³ For we were all baptized by one Spirit into one body—whether Jews or Greeks, whether slaves or free—and we were all made to drink of one Spirit. ¹⁴ So the body is not one part but many. ¹⁵ If the foot should say, "Because I'm not a hand, I don't belong to the body," in spite of this it still belongs to the body. ¹⁶ And if the ear should say, "Because I'm not an eye, I don't belong to the body," in spite of this it still belongs to the body. ¹⁷ If the whole body were an eye, where would the hearing be? If the whole body were an ear, where would the sense of smell be? ¹⁸ But now God has placed each one of the parts in one body just as He wanted. ¹⁹ And if they were all the same part, where would the body be? ²⁰ Now there are many parts, yet one body.

1 CORINTHIANS 12:12-20

Paul then goes on to say that some members of the body can't say, "I don't need you," because that would make as much sense as a parched mouth saying to a pair of hands, "I don't need you to pick up that glass of water for me." The parts not only need to work together but are essential to each other. The word Paul uses is rare in our world; the word is *indispensable*. Paul speaks this surprising word in describing each member of the community of believers and even declares, "The parts of the body that seem to be weaker are indispensable" (1 Cor. 12:22b, ESV).

Some may often feel superior to others and attempt to live life on their own. Others may feel like the weak link, always bringing others down. But Paul insists that all parts of the body, every member in a biblical community, has value and should be considered indispensable. List below specific examples of how you have seen this to be true in your community.

This is a truth that must be grasped to experience the type of community that God designs and desires for those who are His. We must choose to step into our indispensability and recognize and celebrate the indispensability of others. Not only do we need each other in indispensable ways but we are indispensably needed by others—amid all of our flaws, insecurities, strengths, weaknesses, and spiritual gifts.

ONE ANOTHERS

In the group time, we briefly talked about the large number of "one another" verses in Scripture—100 times in the New Testament. Below are just 40 of these verses we find from God's Word. Resist the temptation to skip ahead to the questions. We cannot grow as disciples apart from practicing these mandates with each other in the body of Christ.

1. "Be at peace with one another" (Mark 9:50).
2. "Wash one another's feet" (John 13:14).
3. "Love one another" (John 13:34; 15:12,17).
4. "Show family affection to one another with brotherly love" (Rom. 12:10).
5. "Outdo one another in showing honor" (Rom. 12:10).
6. "Be in agreement with one another" (Rom. 12:16).
7. "Love one another" (Rom. 13:8).
8. "Let us no longer criticize one another" (Rom. 14:13).
9. "Accept one another, just as the Messiah also accepted you" (Rom. 15:7).
10. "Instruct one another" (Rom. 15:14).
11. "When you come together to eat, wait for one another" (1 Cor. 11:33).
12. "Have the same concern for each other" (1 Cor. 12:25).
13. "Serve one another through love" (Gal. 5:13).
14. "We must not become conceited, provoking one another, envying one another" (Gal. 5:26).
15. "Carry one another's burdens" (Gal. 6:2).
16. "With patience, [accept] one another in love" (Eph. 4:2).
17. "Be kind and compassionate to one another" (Eph. 4:32).
18. "Forgiving one another" (Eph. 4:32).
19. Speak "to one another in psalms, hymns and spiritual songs" (Eph. 5:19).
20. Submit "to one another in the fear of Christ" (Eph. 5:21).
21. "In humility consider others as more important yourselves" (Phil. 2:3).
22. "Do not lie to one another" (Col. 3:9).
23. Forgive "one another if anyone has a complaint against another" (Col. 3:13).
24. Teach "one another in all wisdom" (Col. 3:16).
25. Admonish "one another" (Col. 3:16).
26. "May the Lord cause you to increase and overflow with love for one another" (1 Thess. 3:12).
27. "Encourage one another" (1 Thess. 4:18).
28. "Build each other up" (1 Thess. 5:11).
29. "Encourage each other daily" (Heb. 3:13).
30. "Let us be concerned about one another in order to promote love and good works" (Heb. 10:24).

31. "Don't criticize one another" (Jas. 4:11).
32. "Do not complain about one another" (Jas. 5:9).
33. "Confess your sins to one another" (Jas. 5:16).
34. "Pray for one another" (Jas. 5:16).
35. "All of you should be like-minded and sympathetic" (1 Pet. 3:8).
36. "Love believers, and be compassionate and humble" (1 Pet. 3:8).
37. "Maintain an intense love for each other" (1 Pet. 4:8).
38. "Be hospitable to one another without complaining" (1 Pet. 4:9).
39. "Based on the gift each one has received, use it to serve others" (1 Pet. 4:10).
40. "Clothe yourselves with humility toward one another" (1 Pet. 5:5).

Which of these "one anothers" comes naturally to you?

Which of these "one anothers" is tough to apply and why?

What specifically can you learn from and begin to implement into your life in regard to the emphasis Scripture places on community?

John 13:35 says the world will know we are Christians by our love for each other. If a nonbeliever were to observe the relationships within your small group, your ministry team or your church, what would they conclude about Jesus? Are these relationships with other believers marked by the characteristics of Christ or the fruit of His Spirit? When it comes to the communities you are attached to, these are important questions to think about and pray through. We need to constantly have these "one another" verses on our hearts, asking God which verses we need to live out more and in what relationship we need to apply them.

SPIRIT-FILLED LIFE

The Holy Spirit indwells, empowers, and transforms us to live in tune with God

REFLECT

In the previous session we learned that we are all called to live authentically and interdependently with one another in biblical community. Living in proximity with each other isn't enough. Like the root system of the redwood trees, our lives must be interconnected to experience deep biblical community.

Which of the assignments did you explore this week? How did it go?

What did you learn or experience while reading the Bible?

What questions would you like to ask?

PRAY

Begin the session by connecting with God through prayer. Use the following guidelines as you speak with Him:

- Thank God for the Holy Spirit who helps us pray and also intercedes for us when we don't know how to pray for ourselves or for each other.

- Invite the Holy Spirit to guide, teach, and empower your group during discussion.

- Pray that through the power of the Holy Spirit, God will empower us to become more like Jesus.

INTRODUCTION

If you've ever replaced the strings on a guitar you'll notice something. Brand new strings have a tough time staying on pitch. It usually takes a while for the strings to adjust to the correct tension and requires frequent tightening to match the pitch of a tuner. The new strings need to be played often until they can acclimate closer to the correct pitch. After a couple months of regular playing only minor tweaks are needed each day to get the strings in tune. Listening to the tuner and adjusting the strings is always the first step before playing a single note. This must not be skipped if we want to make beautiful music.

In a similar way, before we put our faith in Christ, we were like a hopelessly out-of-tune instrument, incapable of being in sync with the God of the universe. As the Bible points out in Romans 3:23, "all have sinned and fall short of the glory of God." Sin had separated us from God until Jesus Christ saved us through His death, burial, and resurrection. As soon as we receive this gift of grace, we are filled with the Holy Spirit who, like the perfect tuning fork, reveals areas of our lives that need to change and empowers us to be more in tune with God. Over time, as we experience more of God and become increasingly more like Jesus we may need smaller adjustments. However, we will always need to be constantly aligning ourselves with the Spirit's perfect pitch.

Think about an experience when you heard (or sang) something out of tune. What words would you use to describe the effect of such music on you or other listeners?

Share a time, moment, day, or season of life when you sensed you were living in tune with God. Describe the circumstances surrounding this experience.

Throughout Scripture, and most fully in the life of Jesus Christ, we get an accurate picture of what it means to live a life perfectly in tune with God. Yet, we're completely unable to do this on our own. Thankfully, God sent us Jesus to be a model for us and then sent believers the gift of the Holy Spirit to help us become the people He created us to be. It's God's own Spirit that works in and through us to make us more like Jesus. As disciples of Jesus, we can joyfully embrace the reality that God's Spirit dwells within us, empowers us, and transforms us to live in tune with God's desires and plans for us.

KNOW THE STORY

Last week we visited the end of Acts 2 to discover how the early church interacted together in a biblical community. Let's now rewind in the chapter to see what it was that brought this community together.

¹ When the day of Pentecost had arrived, they were all together in one place. ² Suddenly a sound like that of a violent rushing wind came from heaven, and it filled the whole house where they were staying. ³ And tongues, like flames of fire that were divided, appeared to them and rested on each one of them. ⁴ Then they were all filled with the Holy Spirit and began to speak in different languages, as the Spirit gave them ability for speech. ⁵ There were Jews living in Jerusalem, devout men from every nation under heaven. ⁶ When this sound occurred, a crowd came together and was confused because each one heard them speaking in his own language. ⁷ And they were astounded and amazed, saying, "Look, aren't all these who are speaking Galileans? ⁸ How is it that each of us can hear in our own native language? ⁹ Parthians, Medes, Elamites; those who live in Mesopotamia, in Judea and Cappadocia, Pontus and Asia, ¹⁰ Phrygia and Pamphylia, Egypt and the parts of Libya near Cyrene; visitors from Rome, both Jews and proselytes, ¹¹ Cretans and Arabs—we hear them speaking the magnificent acts of God in our own languages." ¹² They were all astounded and perplexed, saying to one another, "What could this be?"
ACTS 2:1-12

What do you find interesting about this account? Why?

What did you observe about the Holy Spirit from this passage?

In this tremendous and awe-inspiring moment in the life of God's people, the "power" that Jesus promised in Acts 1:8 was given to all the believers so that they could be witnesses to the life and love of Jesus "in Jerusalem ... and to the ends of the earth" (Acts 1:8).

UNPACK THE STORY

THE HOLY SPIRIT IN SCRIPTURE

Occurring on the Festival of Pentecost, which was 50 days after Passover, there were religious pilgrims from all over the world who had traveled to Jerusalem to celebrate the event. In Acts 2, the believers spoke in "tongues," or languages, not otherworldly or unintelligible languages. Rather, as Luke recounts the event, people from all nations were able to hear in their own native language all the wonderful things that God had done.

This is a complete reversal of a similar scene in Genesis 11 surrounding the Tower of Babel. At the Tower of Babel, people were fragmented after God confused the language of all the earth as a result of their pride in attempting to build a tower to the heavens to make a name for themselves. Here at Pentecost, people were unified after God made known the gospel in the languages of the people present, which resulted in the believers boasting in the name of Jesus.

Responding to the question asked in Acts 2:12, Peter addressed the swelling crowd. Through the Holy Spirit, people were able to hear the gospel being presented in their own language. As a result, 3,000 people became believers and made the decision to be baptized. In the same way the Gospel of Luke begins with the birth of our Savior, the Acts of the Apostles begins with the birth of the church, setting the stage for the outward ministry explosion ahead. Through the power of the Holy Spirit, the first disciples of Jesus were sent out amid persecution, proclaiming the gospel of Jesus to the ends of the earth.

> **Through the power of the Holy Spirit, the first disciples of Jesus were sent out amid persecution, proclaiming the gospel of Jesus to the ends of the earth.**

If you had been there that day, how do you think you would have responded? Why?

Though the Holy Spirit makes His entrance at the beginning of Acts 2, the Holy Spirit was at work long before that moment at Pentecost. In fact, Scripture describes the relational nature of God as God the Father, God the Spirit, and God the Son. Existing eternally as a distinct member of the Triune Godhead, God's Spirit is present at creation, is the source of life, is our Teacher and Guide, and is the manifestation of God's presence. God's Spirit filled and equipped people in the Old Testament and empowered Jesus' ministry, enabling Him to atone for the sins of the world, judge the world, overthrow the wicked, and reign in justice and righteousness.

THE WORK OF THE HOLY SPIRIT

Jesus spoke often about the Holy Spirit, instructing His disciples to wait for the Holy Spirit since the Spirit was the promise of the Father (see Luke 24:49). Related to this, Jesus on numerous occasions emphasized that it would be God the Father who would send the Spirit to the disciples to teach and remind them of everything that Jesus had already taught.

What is so significant about the events at Pentecost is that every believer since that moment has received the gift of God's Spirit. In the Old Testament, God's Spirit would come and go, but ever since Pentecost, God's Spirit permanently dwells in each believer, signifying that we belong to God.

What does it mean that God's Spirit permanently dwells in us, signifying that we belong to God?

The work of God's Spirit has existed eternally and throughout human history in many active ways, but we also see from Scripture that the Spirit is active in our lives today in a number of ways. Like the early church, each believer receives the Holy Spirit the moment he or she becomes a believer. God's Spirit knows us in our weaknesses, intercedes for us in prayer, helps us understand Scripture, engages us in corporate worship, comforts us during crisis situations, reveals Jesus' purpose for us, reminds us of our identity in Christ, convicts us of our sin, and supports us as we share the gospel with others.

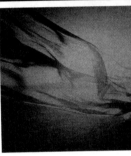

The Holy Spirit also gives individual members of the body of Christ spiritual gifts to build up and empower the church. In the New Testament, we get a picture of the work of the Holy Spirit that individually gifts us but collectively unifies and builds us up to function as the church (see 1 Cor. 12; Eph. 4). Love and unity are given as credible evidence that the Holy Spirit is operating through a group of people, enabling Christ to be revealed in and through us.

> God's Spirit knows us in our weaknesses, intercedes for us in prayer, helps us understand Scripture, ... and supports us as we share the gospel with others.

Review all the ways we can experience the Holy Spirit listed above. Discuss how you have personally experienced the Holy Spirit in some of these examples.

ENGAGE

As a group, identify songs that embody the definition of "great music." After identifying this, take in all of its parts that come together in harmonious ways to create attractive music. Notice how each instrument is in tune with one another, each voice meshes well with the others, and each chord and progression lead to a beautiful unified whole.

After spending some time discussing the qualities of the music you identified, discuss the concept of living "in tune" with God.

What are descriptions of an individual who is "in tune" with God's Spirit?

What are some specific actions a community of believers can carry out that indicate they are collectively "in tune" with the Holy Spirit?

PRAYER REQUESTS

....

....

....

....

....

....

....

....

....

....

....

....

....

In addition to studying God's Word, work with your group leader to create a plan for personal study, worship, and application between now and the next session. Select from the following optional activities to match your personal preferences and available time.

Worship

☐ Read your Bible. Complete the reading plan on page 58.

☐ Spend time with God by engaging the devotional experience on page 59.

☐ Connect with God each day by specifically praying to the Holy Spirit—asking Him to intercede for you, to help you understand Scripture through your reading this week, to reveal Jesus' purposes for you, and to remind you of your identity in Jesus.

Personal Study

☐ Read and interact with "A Study of the Holy Spirit from Paul's Perspective" on page 60.

☐ Read and interact with "The Holy Spirit's Nine-Note Scale" on page 62.

Application

☐ Read Galatians 5:22-23 and identify one person for each of the nine characteristics of the fruit of the Spirit. The goal is to grow in all of these characteristics, but for this activity, think of one person for each of the characteristics listed. Contact each person this week and affirm how you have seen this characteristic displayed in his or her life.

☐ Memorize 2 Corinthians 3:18: "We all, with unveiled faces, are looking as in a mirror at the glory of the Lord and are being transformed into the same image from glory to glory; this is from the Lord who is the Spirit."

☐ Journal your experience. Be aware and take note of all the times you have seen the work of the Spirit this week. This could be from an experience you had sharing the gospel with someone. It could be during your time alone with God in prayer and Scripture reading. You may also take note of how you experienced the Spirit during a time of corporate worship.

☐ Other:

 **WORSHIP**

READING PLAN

Read through the following Scripture passages this week. Use the space provided to record your thoughts and responses.

Day 1
John 14:25-26

Day 2
Ephesians 5:18-20

Day 3
2 Corinthians 3:7-18

Day 4
Romans 8:18-27

Day 5
Ezekiel 36:22-38

Day 6
John 16:5-15

Day 7
Galatians 5:16-26

IN TUNE

An essential element of music isn't only notes that are in tune but also rhythm that is consistent. By definition, sound without rhythm is noise. Sadly, many of our lives are lived at such a frantic and hurried pace that the sound of our lives is more akin to noise rather than music. The God who is revealed in Scripture is a God of rhythm. We see this clearly in the Genesis 1 creation account where the description of all things being created happens in six days followed by a day of rest. Much more beautiful than just noise, God created everything and according to Zephaniah 3:17, He rejoices over His people with singing.

We were created for a rhythm that lines up with God's rhythm. It's from a place of rest that the music of our lives comes forth. Look at some of the following passages that address seeking out a place of rest and peace in your life by staying in tune with the Spirit and in rhythm with God the Father.

> 12 Moses said to the LORD, "Look, You have told me, 'Lead this people up,' but You have not let me know whom You will send with me. You said, 'I know you by name, and you have also found favor in My sight.' 13 Now if I have indeed found favor in Your sight, please teach me Your ways, and I will know You and find favor in Your sight. Now consider that this nation is Your people." 14 Then He replied, "My presence will go with you, and I will give you rest."
> **EXODUS 33:12-14**

> 28 "Come to Me, all of you who are weary and burdened, and I will give you rest. 29 All of you, take up My yoke and learn from Me, because I am gentle and humble in heart, and you will find rest for yourselves. 30 For My yoke is easy and My burden is light."
> **MATTHEW 11:28-30**

> Now may the God of hope fill you with all joy and peace as you believe in Him so that you may overflow with hope by the power of the Holy Spirit.
> **ROMANS 15:13**

In the same way, choose to begin adjusting the rhythm of your life in small, tangible ways. Perhaps you might start each day from the restful place of prayer or Scripture reading before you begin to read your emails or pick up your phone. It may be a daily or weekly conversation you initiate between a friend or a family member, talking through how you've experienced God lately. Whatever small step you choose, pray that God's Spirit will guide it to a healthy and soul-enriching rhythm in your life.

A STUDY OF THE HOLY SPIRIT FROM PAUL'S PERSPECTIVE

Paul made attempts to live in tune with God's design and desire. In Philippians 3:4-6, he even says that according to the law he was "blameless." However, Paul's conclusion was that all these things added up to "filth" (v. 8). In other words, he was living out of tune. However, he didn't realize he was living out of tune until he encountered Jesus in all of His perfection. As a result, Paul was willing to trade his "out of tune" life for knowing Jesus "and the power of His resurrection" (v. 10). Then, the rest of Paul's life was an ongoing journey of tuning and re-tuning his life through the power of the Holy Spirit. Like Paul, we can choose to live either in tune or out of tune, in harmony or in cacophony.

> *In the same way Paul came to the conclusion he was living a life out of tune with God, describe a time when you realized you were living out of tune.*

> *What spiritual disciplines, relationships, or experiences have helped you get back in alignment or help keep you in alignment with God?*

As Paul was on a journey of living in tune with God through the power of the Holy Spirit, he taught and equipped others to do the same. In his missionary journeys and letters to the churches, we see some of his teaching that reminds us of the Holy Spirit's integral role in living in tune as individuals and as a community of disciples.

In 2 Corinthians 3:18 he writes that "We all, with unveiled faces, are looking as in a mirror at the glory of the Lord and are being transformed into the same image from glory to glory; this is from the Lord who is the Spirit." In other words, through the Holy Spirit we are continually being fine tuned to become more like Jesus. Though we can't live in tune on our own power, through God's Spirit, our lives will begin to resonate more and more with Jesus who lived a life perfectly in tune. God never gives up on us and His Spirit is constantly at work empowering and guiding us.

What words or emotions come to mind when you learn that God is continually tuning your life to become more like Jesus?

As we well know, there are things in our lives that can quickly cause us to get out of tune. In Galatians 5:17 Paul writes, "For the flesh desires what is against the Spirit, and the Spirit desires what is against the flesh; these are opposed to each other, so that you don't do what you want."

Paul goes on to list two different ways of living: works of the flesh and fruit of the Spirit. To paraphrase, these two different ways of living are not compatible and can never be in harmony with one another. A life filled with works of the flesh—such as envy, anger, and jealousy—will always clash with a life filled with fruit of the Spirit—such as joy, love, and self-control.

Though we might choose to live by the Spirit, works of the flesh will continue to be a temptation in our lives. There will most likely be moments or even seasons where we stop listening or obeying God and get out of tune. It's essential that we don't give up on the journey that God is committed to in our lives.

In Philippians 1:6, Paul writes: "I am sure of this, that He who started a good work in you will carry it on to completion until the day of Christ Jesus." In other words, God always finishes what He starts. No matter how difficult or out of tune you may feel as a disciple of Jesus, God will complete that work in and through you until the day you are face to face with Christ.

Tuning an instrument is critical to making music, especially in combination with other instruments. As you think through this week of study thus far, how does the Holy Spirit help us be in tune with God's purposes and desires for us?

THE HOLY SPIRIT'S NINE-NOTE SCALE

The apostle Paul's metaphor of "the fruit of the Spirit" could be paraphrased to "notes of the Spirit" as a way to describe the sound of a life that is "in tune" with God. Living a life that is in tune with the Holy Spirit is to resonate the nine-note scale of love, joy, peace, patience, kindness, goodness, faithfulness, gentleness, and self-control as described in Galatians 5:22-23. To tune our lives to anything other than the Spirit is to live "off key." Our lives, like instruments, desperately need the true pitch of the Holy Spirit as our tuning fork.

An easy test to see if we are out of tune is to reflect on the words, thoughts, and actions in our lives, while at the same time considering the nine-note scale from the Spirit. If our lives are out of tune, then there is something other than the Holy Spirit resonating within us. Sometimes it is fear, anxiety, pride, lack of trust, or an inability to remember who God is and who God created us to be that causes us to get out of tune. As a follower of Jesus, we have God's Spirit dwelling inside of us and we can make the choice to cooperate with the Spirit in "re-tuning" so that our lives better resonate with the fullness of His Spirit.

As you consider whether your words, thoughts, and actions are in tune with God's Spirit, examine each of the following in the nine-note scale of the Holy Spirit.

Love: "Love is patient, love is kind. Love does not envy, is not boastful, is not conceited, does not act improperly, is not selfish, is not provoked, and does not keep a record of wrongs. Love finds no joy in unrighteousness but rejoices in the truth. It bears all things, believes all things, hopes all things, endures all things" (1 Cor. 13:4-7).

Joy: "Now may the God of hope fill you with all joy and peace as you believe in Him so that you may overflow with hope by the power of the Holy Spirit" (Rom. 15:13).

Peace: "I have told you these things so that in Me you may have peace. You will have suffering in this world. Be courageous! I have conquered the world" (John 16:33).

Patience: "Be patient, therefore, brothers, until the coming of the Lord. See how the farmer waits for the precious fruit of the earth, being patient about it, until it receives the early and the late rains" (Jas. 5:7).

Kindness: "And be kind and compassionate to one another, forgiving one another, just as God also forgave you in Christ" (Eph. 4:32).

Goodness: "Therefore, as we have opportunity, we must work for the good of all, especially for those who belong to the household of faith" (Gal. 6:10).

Faithfulness: "Whoever is faithful in very little is also faithful in much, and whoever is unrighteous in very little is also unrighteous in much" (Luke 16:10).

Gentleness: "To slander no one, to avoid fighting, and to be kind, always showing gentleness to all people" (Titus 3:2).

Self-control: "Instructing us to deny godlessness and worldly lusts and to live in a sensible, righteous, and godly way in the present age" (Titus 2:12).

Choose one of the nine fruits of the Spirit that God is currently growing within you. Give an example of how you have seen the Spirit changing your thoughts, perspective, attitude, or behavior in that area of your life.

What is one of the characteristics listed in Galatians 5:22-23 that you would like to reflect more in your life? What simple and practical steps could you take this week to cooperate with God in further developing that attribute? (For example, if you would like to grow in patience, you might consider letting cars merge in front of you in traffic or allowing people to move ahead of you in line when you get coffee or at the grocery store.)

SERVING HIS KINGDOM

Disciples serve Jesus by expending time, talents, and resources in His kingdom.

REFLECT

We examined in the previous session how God sent us Jesus to show us the way and then sent believers the gift of the Holy Spirit to help us become the people He created us to be. We saw that it is God's own Spirit that works in and through us to make us more like Jesus. Because of this, we can be encouraged that God's Spirit dwells within us, empowers us, and transforms us to live in tune with God's desires and plans for us.

Which of the assignments did you explore this week? How did it go?

What did you learn or experience while reading the Bible?

What questions would you like to ask?

PRAY

Begin the session by connecting with God through prayer. Use the following guidelines as you speak with Him:

- Ask God to guide your discussion about what it means to serve His kingdom.

- Pray that God would open up our hearts and minds to what it looks like for us to fully invest in building God's kingdom rather than our own kingdoms.

- Thank God that when Jesus returns and establishes His kingdom here, all earthly kingdoms, death, and destruction will be defeated permanently.

- Pray that because of this future hope, it will affect how we serve the kingdom today.

INTRODUCTION

Every street surrounding every new car dealership in America has something in common; every day on that street, tens of thousands of dollars simply vanish. There's no getting around it, stopping it, or avoiding it. The dealerships, the police, and the public haven't been able to do anything about it. So, what's so unique about every street surrounding every new car dealership in America that causes it to hemorrhage money? Depreciation.

On average, every new car that has just been purchased will decline in value approximately 9 percent the moment its new driver takes it off the lot. In other words, every year, roughly 15 million new car owners spend money on something that loses money as quickly as it's spent. This isn't just true with cars. It's true with almost everything we spend money on. Depreciation is an inescapable phenomenon for most purchases. Accountants even have a line item in spreadsheets to track the depreciation of assets for an individual, family business, or for a multi-national corporation. Depreciation is so common that we've even come up with tax incentives where depreciation can be "written off" because it's considered an expense, a cost of life.

There are some objects such as rare cars, unique collectibles, or unusual art that actually increase in value over time. Yet, a rare car could lose value after a hail storm damages it, a rare baseball card could lose value if the player is exposed for a scandal, and a piece of art could lose value if a huge collection from the same artist was discovered nullifying its rarity. Virtually everything we spend money on will either begin depreciating in value immediately or at some point down the road.

However, there is one thing that is guaranteed not to depreciate in value: God's kingdom.

What is your most valuable possession? What makes it valuable?

If you didn't have this thing, how would your life be different? How would not having this effect your eternal existence?

Jesus said that when we expend our lives in God's kingdom, there is nothing that can destroy, diminish, or even steal our investment (see Matt. 6:19-21). In this session we will consider what the kingdom of God is and how we, as disciples, are called to serve as Jesus did by spending our time, talents, energies, and resources in the most rewarding and permanent venture in history: the movement of God's kingdom.

KNOW THE STORY

There is a man in Scripture who is famous for what he held onto and it challenges us still today.

> 18 A ruler asked Him, "Good Teacher, what must I do to inherit eternal life?" 19 "Why do you call Me good?" Jesus asked him. "No one is good but One—God. 20 You know the commandments: Do not commit adultery; do not murder; do not steal; do not bear false witness; honor your father and mother." 21 "I have kept all these from my youth," he said. 22 When Jesus heard this, He told him, "You still lack one thing: Sell all that you have and distribute it to the poor, and you will have treasure in heaven. Then come, follow Me." 23 After he heard this, he became extremely sad, because he was very rich. 24 Seeing that he became sad, Jesus said, "How hard it is for those who have wealth to enter the kingdom of God! 25 For it is easier for a camel to go through the eye of a needle than for a rich person to enter the kingdom of God." 26 Those who heard this asked, "Then who can be saved?" 27 He replied, "What is impossible with men is possible with God." 28 Then Peter said, "Look, we have left what we had and followed You." 29 So He said to them, "I assure you: There is no one who has left a house, wife or brothers, parents or children because of the kingdom of God, 30 who will not receive many times more at this time, and eternal life in the age to come."
>
> **LUKE 18:18-30**

According to Luke's account, this man not only had great wealth, but he was also a moral, religious leader. He had everything—yet his heart was still restless. He appears to be sincere in asking Jesus about the one thing he lacked—eternal life. The assurance of eternal life would have completed his portfolio and his sense of security. Jesus, able to perceive the intentions of this man, cuts to the heart of the matter. Jesus instructs him to do the one thing that he has yet to do: sell everything and give it to the poor so that he can follow Him. Jesus wasn't condemning the wealth of this man but rather was confronting a heart that was wrapped up in his possessions. Sadly, this man walked away, holding onto what he thought was treasure, not allowing his hands and his heart to grasp the true treasure in front of him—Jesus.

Can you relate to this man? What attitudes or fears may have prompted him to choose wealth and a religious life over Jesus?

UNPACK THE STORY

THE KINGDOM OF GOD

At the end of this story in Luke, we see that this rich young ruler served and invested in himself rather than serving the King and investing in His kingdom. In doing so, he missed the chance to hold onto the very thing that would finally fulfill his restless heart.

Share a time when you were faced with a choice to serve yourself or to serve God. What did you give up? What did you gain?

We see from Genesis through Revelation amazing examples of God exercising His rule and reign in different ways.

The kingdom of God is an integral truth not only within Jesus' teaching but also within the larger framework of the entire biblical narrative. Scripture also refers to the "kingdom of heaven," the "kingdom of the Lord," the "kingdom of Christ," and simply the "kingdom." These are all just different ways to point to the same thing. Namely, there is an active reign of God that is experienced differently throughout history and throughout the universe. The kingdom of God is wherever and whenever God is allowed to rule and reign. We see from Genesis through Revelation amazing examples of God exercising His rule and reign in different ways.

We see this all the way at the beginning in Genesis when, through the power of God's word, all things in the universe were created, and God described it all as "very good" (Gen. 1:31). In the garden of Eden, we experienced the wholeness that came from God ruling over us. However, we rebelled against God and placed ourselves on the throne of our own hearts. We rejected God as King, and we lost the experience of thriving in God's kingdom. In doing so, human kingdoms were established that were the complete antithesis of the experience of God's kingdom. There was injustice, exploitation, discord, insecurity, and so much more. In contrast, God's reign and rule are unlike any other authority, power, or earthly ruler. Unlike other earthly kingdoms, God's kingdom is marked by peace, joy, love, prosperity, security, and significance among many other things.

When we pray "Your kingdom come" from the Lord's Prayer, what are we essentially asking of God (Matt. 6:10)?

What are some evidences of God's kingdom at work in our lives and in the lives of other disciples around us?

OUR PLACE IN GOD'S KINGDOM

When Jesus came to earth, He inaugurated a new and permanent reality of the kingdom of God. Wherever Jesus went, God's kingdom was experienced. It was an already present reality. Sins were forgiven, the blind received sight, and the sick were miraculously healed. Those on the margins of society were embraced, and even the dead were raised to life. God's reign and rule were active and present in Jesus' life. Furthermore, Jesus invites His followers to be ambassadors and agents for God's kingdom work. We've been invited to experience life with Jesus as King and to serve and invest in God's kingdom, both individually and corporately.

What would it look like for us to invest more fully in building God's kingdom rather than our own kingdoms? Share specific examples of using our time, resources, and skills differently.

Whenever we participate in God's kingdom work by putting into practice Jesus' teaching through the power of the Holy Spirit, we are able to experience the present reality of God being King in our lives. In many ways, the kingdom of God has drastically different values than kingdoms of this world. Enemies are loved, the marginalized are brought in, the meek inherit the earth, the weak members of the community are described as indispensable, and humble service is the greatest display of power. It's no wonder that Jesus says, "seek first the kingdom of God" (Matt. 6:33).

However, there is also a future reality of God's kingdom that has yet to be realized. When Jesus returns and establishes His kingdom here, all earthly kingdoms, death, and destruction will be defeated permanently. What we experience now in regard to living as citizens of heaven is just an appetizer to the brilliant banquet that is our future inheritance as the people of God, living eternally in God's presence in the new heavens and new earth. Because of this future hope, it also affects how we live today. As the apostle Paul wrote in 1 Corinthians 15:58, "Therefore, my dear brothers, be steadfast, immovable, always excelling in the Lord's work, knowing that your labor in the Lord is not in vain."

> We've been invited to experience life with Jesus as King and to serve and invest in God's kingdom, both individually and corporately.

How can a future reality motivate us to give ourselves fully to the work of the Lord today?

ENGAGE

Since Jesus is extravagantly generous and gracious with us, let us follow His model in a tangible way by being generous with others. As a group, decide how you can be Jesus' hands and feet. Use the time remaining to brainstorm ideas to serve the kingdom of God as a group. Don't just talk about it; make a plan to carry it out. Below are some options to get you started.

- Provide meals for someone in need.

- Clean up the yard of a neighbor, a single parent family, or a senior citizen.

- Make lunches for the homeless at your local shelter or food pantry.

- Create a "Serve Day" as a group and find someone in need inside or outside of the church.

- Collect money as a group to help someone who is struggling financially, for a mission trip that someone in the church is raising money for, or for a family seeking support for an upcoming adoption.

PRAYER REQUESTS

....

....

....

....

....

....

....

....

....

....

....

....

In addition to studying God's Word, work with your group leader to create a plan for personal study, worship, and application between now and the next session. Select from the following optional activities to match your personal preferences and available time.

↑ Worship

☑ Read your Bible. Complete the reading plan on page 72.

☐ Spend time with God by engaging the devotional experience on page 73.

☐ Connect with God each day through prayer asking Him to show you areas in your life that you can give for the sake of the kingdom.

➡ ⬅ Personal Study

☐ Read and interact with "The Kingdom of God" on page 74.

☐ Read and interact with "Our Place in God's Kingdom" on page 76.

⬅ ➡ Application

☐ Take some time this week to read and ponder Matthew 13:10-50. Spend time in prayer and journaling, considering the many ways in which our King describes His kingdom.

☐ Consider giving a small sum of money anonymously to someone in need, paying for a student's scholarship for Christian camp, or paying for the food of the car behind you at a fast-food restaurant.

☐ Memorize Matthew 6:33: "But seek first the kingdom of God and His righteousness, and all these things will be provided for you."

☐ Other:

 **WORSHIP**

READING PLAN

Read through the following Scripture passages this week. Use the space provided to record your thoughts and responses.

Day 1
1 Corinthians 15:50-58

Day 2
Mark 10:35-45

Day 3
1 Peter 4:1-11

Day 4
Galatians 5:1-15

Day 5
John 13:12-20

Day 6
Matthew 25:31-46

Day 7
Philippians 2:1-11

"IS LIKE"

The kingdom of God is so expansive and wondrous that Jesus never defined it in a sound bite. Rather, He invited people to have eyes that would see things that only come through faith in Jesus, empowered by the Holy Spirit, as we continually refocus on the things that matter most to Jesus. Of the many ways in which Jesus invited others to see, taste, experience, encounter, and expend their lives on the kingdom of God, one of Jesus' frequent methods was to paint word pictures by telling "is like" stories.

For example, here are a few "is like" stories that help frame our perspective of Jesus' kingdom:

> "The kingdom of heaven is like a man who sowed good seed in his field" (Matt. 13:24, NIV).

> "The kingdom of heaven is like a mustard seed" (Matt. 13:31).

> "The kingdom of heaven is like yeast that a woman took and mixed into 50 pounds of flour until it spread through all of it" (Matt. 13:33).

> "The kingdom of heaven is like treasure, buried in a field" (Matt. 13:44).

> "The kingdom of heaven is like a net that was let down into the lake and caught all kinds of fish" (Matt. 13:47, NIV).

> "The kingdom of heaven is like a king who wanted to settle accounts with his servants" (Matt. 18:23, NIV).

> "The kingdom of heaven is like a landowner who went out early in the morning to hire workers for his vineyard" (Matt. 20:1).

> "The kingdom of heaven is like a king who prepared a wedding banquet for his son" (Matt. 22:2, NIV).

For those looking for a sound bite definition of the kingdom so that it can be quantified and consumed, Jesus' approach is frustrating. And yet, Jesus asks loud enough for us to hear, "How can we illustrate the kingdom of God, or what parable can we use to describe it?" (Mark 4:30). It's as if Jesus is inviting us to explore the kingdom with Him. He invites us to experience it and to expend our lives on it. We could spend the rest of our lives exploring it as we put Jesus' teaching into practice and we would still not grasp the fullness of God's kingdom.

THE KINGDOM OF GOD

The concepts of a kingdom and a king are foreign to most of us in the United States. Yet, we have many examples from history and popular culture of kings and kingdoms.

In the space below, describe some attributes of a kingdom and some characteristics of a king, both good and bad.

How does this metaphor help you understand God's kingdom and God at work in our world?

Consider the city in which you live. Could you describe it in one sentence? If you try, what about the restaurants you forgot to mention. What about the mayor who didn't quite make it in the description? How about the parks, the schools, and the residents? What about the street names, the plant names, and the shop names? Did you remember to include the elevation? The population? The average temperature in the summer? You see, to reduce the enormous complexity of even the smallest city into just one simple sound bite is to attempt the impossible.

If instead, you began to experience the city, walk the streets, meet the residents, patronize the shops, eat the food, get lost and ask for directions, sit still as the shadows get longer at the end of the day, walk barefoot across the grass dew in the park at sunrise—then you might get a glimpse of what your city is. Truth be told, a lifetime in a city still isn't enough to grasp the fullness of it.

Infinitely more is the task of grasping the kingdom of God. And yet, Jesus says that children are better equipped at experiencing it (see Mark 10:15). Perhaps there is a sense of awe and wonder that we grow out of as we mature into adulthood that is the necessary variable in experiencing God's kingdom.

What keeps many people from giving themselves fully to serving Jesus, the King of kings?

What choices can you make to serve the kingdom today?

Read each of the following passages and note what each says about the kingdom.

Matthew 6:31-33

John 18:33-38

Luke 17:20-21

There is no greater investment with our time, talents, and treasure than investing in the kingdom of God, "where neither moth nor rust destroys, and where thieves don't break in and steal," and where we find at the center of it all the most valuable treasure of all—Jesus (Matt. 6:20).

➡️ ⬅️ PERSONAL STUDY 2

OUR PLACE IN GOD'S KINGDOM

Every kingdom has a king. Thankfully, there is none like King Jesus. He is a humble King, a mighty King, a righteous King, a faithful King, a just King, a merciful King, and so much more. The more you get to know Jesus as King, the more you will experience and learn about His kingdom.

We see a glimpse of Jesus as King in Matthew 25, but it may not be what you expect. We find our King identifying Himself with "the least of these"—the hungry, the thirsty, the stranger, the naked, the sick, and the imprisoned.

31 "When the Son of Man comes in His glory, and all the angels with Him, then He will sit on the throne of His glory. 32 All the nations will be gathered before Him, and He will separate them one from another, just as a shepherd separates the sheep from the goats. 33 He will put the sheep on His right and the goats on the left. 34 Then the King will say to those on His right, 'Come, you who are blessed by My Father, inherit the kingdom prepared for you from the foundation of the world. 35 For I was hungry and you gave Me something to eat; I was thirsty and you gave Me something to drink; I was a stranger and you took Me in; 36 I was naked and you clothed Me; I was sick and you took care of Me; I was in prison and you visited Me.' 37 "Then the righteous will answer Him, 'Lord, when did we see You hungry and feed You, or thirsty and give You something to drink? 38 When did we see You a stranger and take You in, or without clothes and clothe You? 39 When did we see You sick, or in prison, and visit You?' 40 "And the King will answer them, 'I assure you: Whatever you did for one of the least of these brothers of Mine, you did for Me.' 41 Then He will also say to those on the left, 'Depart from Me, you who are cursed, into the eternal fire prepared for the Devil and his angels! 42 For I was hungry and you gave Me nothing to eat; I was thirsty and you gave Me nothing to drink; 43 I was a stranger and you didn't take Me in; I was naked and you didn't clothe Me, sick and in prison and you didn't take care of Me.' 44 "Then they too will answer, 'Lord, when did we see You hungry, or thirsty, or a stranger, or without clothes, or sick, or in prison, and not help You?' 45 "Then He will answer them, 'I assure you: Whatever you did not do for one of the least of these, you did not do for Me either.' 46 "And they will go away into eternal punishment, but the righteous into eternal life."
MATTHEW 25:31-46

Who do you most identify with: the sheep or the goat? Why?

Jesus clearly lays out in this parable how we are to love, care for, and serve one another—especially the disadvantaged. Jesus also doesn't stand back at a distance and give these instructions without first giving Himself as an example. Throughout the New Testament, we find Jesus serving and helping those in need. And He also taught this to His disciples.

> [42] Jesus called them over and said to them, "You know that those who are regarded as rulers of the Gentiles dominate them, and their men of high positions exercise power over them. [43] But it must not be like that among you. On the contrary, whoever wants to become great among you must be your servant, [44] and whoever wants to be first among you must be a slave to all. [45] For even the Son of Man did not come to be served, but to serve, and to give His life—a ransom for many."
> **MARK 10:42-45**

Jesus models for us a life of constant service to different kinds of people in various types of situations, and He expects the same from us. We love one another because Christ loved us. We serve one another because Christ served us. We sacrifice and die to our comforts and conveniences for the sake of others because Christ sacrificed His life for our sake on the cross.

Are there specific types of people you find easier to serve? What are some types of service that you enjoy providing for others? Explain.

How can you stretch yourself this week by serving outside your comfort zone? Write out a plan below.

SPREADING THE GOOD NEWS

As disciples, we are sent by Jesus to
embody the good news of the gospel
with both our words and our lives.

REFLECT

In Session 5, we discussed what the kingdom of God is and how we, as disciples, are called to serve as Jesus did by spending our time, talents, energies, and resources in the most rewarding and permanent venture in history. Because Jesus models for us a life of constant service to different kinds of people in various types of situations, He expects the same from us. We love one another because Christ loved us. We serve one another because Christ served us. We sacrifice and die to our comforts and conveniences for the sake of others because Christ sacrificed His life for our sake on the cross.

Which of the assignments did you explore this week? How did it go?

What did you learn or experience while reading the Bible?

What questions would you like to ask?

PRAY

Begin the session by connecting with God through prayer. Use the following guidelines as you speak with Him:

- Ask God to give your group the heart to be Great Commission disciple-makers. "Go, therefore, and make disciples of all nations" (Matt. 28:19).

- Pray that even before you begin discussing this session that God would place the names of unbelievers on your hearts and minds.

- Ask God to give each group member the boldness and wisdom to share his or her own story of faith.

- Pray that God will give your group the ears to listen, the hearts to love, the hands to serve, and the words to speak both grace and truth to these people.

INTRODUCTION

Everyone loves to get good news. Whether it is from a friend, spouse, teacher, boss, doctor, or mechanic, good news is always received with a warm welcome. But why is it that the gospel, which literally means "good news," can be so difficult for us to share? Why does it stir up feelings of inadequacy, stress, obligation, anxiety, and fear of rejection? Perhaps we have forgotten that the good news of the gospel is actually the greatest news that has ever been delivered.

What good news have you received recently? What made it good, and how did it impact you?

Sometimes words become so familiar, they lose their meaning, becoming instead an altered, assumed, or powerless term. The word *gospel* is one of those words. If you asked a hundred Christians to explain what *gospel* means, you might get a hundred different answers. In the same way, since "to evangelize" literally means, "to be a messenger of the gospel," you may likely hear many diverse definitions of *evangelism*.

In this session, we will provide a pathway for evangelism that is both narrow and broad. It's narrow because it's only and always about Jesus. It's broad because the good news about the gospel has both personal and cosmic ramifications. Those three words—Jesus, personal, and cosmic—hold together the richness, beauty, and power of the gospel that Jesus has empowered us to embody with our words and our lives. When we allow the good news of the gospel to penetrate deep into our hearts, we are then propelled to share that same good news with others.

How would you define "the gospel" in one sentence?

What thoughts and emotions are stirred up when you hear the word "evangelism"?

KNOW THE STORY

Perhaps one of the most fascinating accounts of evangelism in the Bible is found in Acts 17. Luke records in extraordinary detail how apostle Paul shared the good news of Jesus to the Greeks in a way that was both personal and cosmic at the same time. As you read this passage, pay attention to details from his description of this scene. Underline words or phrases that either stand out as significant, surprising, or needing further explanation. Then spend some time discussing these things.

22 Then Paul stood in the middle of the Areopagus and said: "Men of Athens! I see that you are extremely religious in every respect. 23 For as I was passing through and observing the objects of your worship, I even found an altar on which was inscribed: TO AN UNKNOWN GOD. Therefore, what you worship in ignorance, this I proclaim to you. 24 The God who made the world and everything in it—He is Lord of heaven and earth and does not live in shrines made by hands. 25 Neither is He served by human hands, as though He needed anything, since He Himself gives everyone life and breath and all things. 26 From one man He has made every nationality to live over the whole earth and has determined their appointed times and the boundaries of where they live. 27 He did this so they might seek God, and perhaps they might reach out and find Him, though He is not far from each one of us. 28 For in Him we live and move and exist, as even some of your own poets have said, 'For we are also His offspring.' 29 Being God's offspring then, we shouldn't think that the divine nature is like gold or silver or stone, an image fashioned by human art and imagination. 30 "Therefore, having overlooked the times of ignorance, God now commands all people everywhere to repent, 31 because He has set a day when He is going to judge the world in righteousness by the Man He has appointed. He has provided proof of this to everyone by raising Him from the dead."
ACTS 17:22-31

What did you underline or highlight from this passage?
What stood out as significant, surprising, or needing further explanation?

UNPACK THE STORY

EVANGELISM IS NARROW

In light of this passage, let's consider the three words mentioned in the introduction as a way to understand Paul's method of evangelism: Jesus, personal, and cosmic.

Jesus: For Paul, and for us, it's always and only all about Jesus. The gospel is defined entirely by the reality of Jesus' life and work. The fullness of Jesus' life extends all the way back into eternity past (see John 17:1-5), extends into eternity future (see Rev. 21:1-7), and is the subject of the entire Bible.

God's personal and cosmic answer to the question "What is the gospel?" can be summarized in one name: Jesus. He is our only hope to be reconciled to God. Only in Jesus do we find lasting peace, justice, and satisfaction. Through Jesus, we are redeemed, renewed, and restored. And this is why evangelism is narrow—because it's only and always about Jesus.

> Only in Jesus do we find lasting peace, justice, and satisfaction. Through Jesus, we are redeemed, renewed, and restored.

Discuss for a moment some of the things we would miss if we attempted to share the gospel with someone while failing to include Jesus. Why is Jesus so important to this good news?

The apostle Paul was in Athens because the good news about Jesus had completely captured his heart and mind, causing Paul to leave his life of religious legalism and embrace a liberating relationship with God through faith in Jesus. Paul was willing to go to the ends of the earth and endure all things, not to earn God's love but because God's love extended to him through Jesus. Though Paul spent much of his time in Athens talking about a variety of things, the motivation for all of his words was to lead people directly to Jesus.

Who shared the gospel with you? What did they do or say that was persuasive and moved you toward Jesus?

Was there anything they did or said that was unhelpful and moved you away from Jesus? Briefly explain.

EVANGELISM IS BROAD

Evangelism is also broad because the gospel has both personal and cosmic ramifications.

Personal: Acts 17 is just one of many passages that reminds us that the good news of the gospel has personal implications. In fact, the gospel is so personal that it transcends every culture, every nation, every language, and every unique human experience and can be delivered to every person on earth on a first name basis. The life that Jesus lived and the work that He accomplished are not just impersonal loopholes that can get us out of hell if we just believe in Jesus. Rather, the life and work of Jesus were accomplished with us in mind, His cherished children, as well as every other human being.

This is why apostle Paul starts off by making observations about the lives of those in Athens. He wants to communicate the gospel in words that they would personally understand. Paul even goes so far to quote two poems about the Greek god Zeus as he shares the gospel. Though he uses words he's never used before, he's pointing directly to the same, unchanging Jesus who is the only way to the Father. As a result, at least two individuals, as recorded by Luke, embraced the good news about Jesus that day.

Why is it important to understand the culture, values, experiences, and perspectives of those with whom we are sharing the gospel?

Cosmic: While the good news of the gospel has personal ramifications, it also affects everything in all of creation. Acts 17:24-27 records Paul describing God as the Creator and Sustainer of all things, the Mover of history, and the One who desires people to reach out to Him. The good news of the gospel is twofold: (1) Jesus redeems and reconciles every person who puts his or her faith in Jesus; and (2) Jesus is reconciling and restoring all things on earth and in the heavens. Though Paul delivers the message of the gospel personally to those in Athens, he reminds them that the work God is accomplishing through Jesus is beyond the largest scale imaginable.

The gospel is so personal that it transcends every culture, every nation, every language, and every unique human experience.

In your opinion, why is it unimaginable that Jesus longs to redeem, reconcile, and restore us?

ENGAGE

In the space provided below, draw a basic sketch of your street, apartment building, or workplace. Label each house, door, or cubical with the name of the person, or people, who live there. Mark those you know to be followers of Jesus, other religious affiliations, and those who you don't yet know.

Spend some time brainstorming as a group some ideas of how you might share Christ through words or acts of service. For example, you might consider having an "Acts 17 Party" and invite neighbors, coworkers, and friends to a potluck or barbeque with your small group. Inviting these people into your home to hang out with you and your group is a great way for them to experience the love of Christ.

When you are done brainstorming ideas, pair up with one other person in the group. Share the sketch with each other and pray together for God's Spirit to work in you and in each person on the sketch.

PRAYER REQUESTS

....

....

....

....

....

....

....

In addition to studying God's Word, work with your group leader to create a plan for personal study, worship, and application between now and the next session. Select from the following optional activities to match your personal preferences and available time.

↑ Worship

☑ Read your Bible. Complete the reading plan on page 86.

☐ Spend time with God by engaging the devotional experience on page 87.

☐ Identify three people in your life who you would like to share the good news of Jesus Christ with and pray for each of them that God would give you ears to listen, a heart to love, hands to serve, and words to speak both grace and truth.

➡ ⬅ Personal Study

☐ Read and interact with "The Gospel Always Points to Jesus" on page 88.

☐ Read and interact with "Romans Road" on page 90.

⬅ ➡ Application

☐ Memorize Romans 10:15b: "How beautiful are the feet of those who announce the gospel of good things!"

☐ Pay attention to conversations you have this week. Journal about all of those conversation and how you could transition into the a sharing of your faith in each. Attempt to give as many transitions as possible.

☐ Share your faith in Jesus with at least one person this week. This may be intimidating, but remember that you don't need to give a speech or attempt to convince people in any way. You just need to tell your faith story simply and sincerely, with love for the person with whom you share it.

☐ Other:

WORSHIP

READING PLAN

Read through the following Scripture passages this week. Use the space provided to record your thoughts and responses.

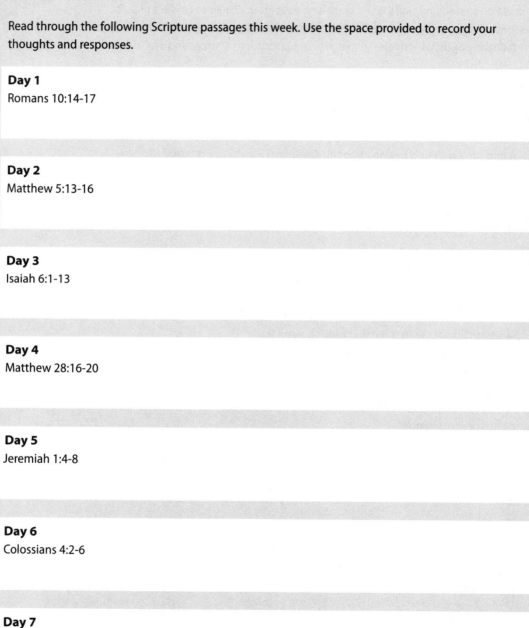

Day 1
Romans 10:14-17

Day 2
Matthew 5:13-16

Day 3
Isaiah 6:1-13

Day 4
Matthew 28:16-20

Day 5
Jeremiah 1:4-8

Day 6
Colossians 4:2-6

Day 7
1 Peter 3:13-22

YOUR STORY

The good news of Jesus' life and work is that it has personal ramifications for you, along with everyone else. And though it's easy to forget, you are the world's foremost expert when it comes to describing your life and how you have experienced the good news of Jesus. There is no seminary professor, pastor, teacher, or leader who is more qualified to speak about your life than you are.

In 1 Peter 3:15, you are reminded that you should "always be ready to give a defense to anyone who asks you for a reason for the hope that is in you." Consider this an opportunity to get ready for a future moment when you can share your story with someone who is curious about how you have experienced Jesus.

Take some time to put into words how you have experienced this good news so that you can readily share with others when asked about the hope that is in you that flows from a relationship with Jesus. Use the questions below as you craft your story.

How did your relationship with Jesus free you from striving to earn God's approval?

How did Jesus free you from a particular sin or addiction?

How did Jesus change your perspective even though your circumstances stayed the same?

How did Jesus give meaning to your life, give you hope, give you peace, or set you free from the bondage of a guilty conscience?

 **PERSONAL STUDY**

THE GOSPEL ALWAYS POINTS TO JESUS

If you explored every New Testament account of the disciples of Jesus sharing the good news about Jesus to others, you'd quickly find there is no formulaic speech delivered. In fact, since no two evangelistic accounts are exactly the same, it's a great reminder that the gospel is far more personal than a program. However, every telling of the good news has one thing in common: it always points to Jesus.

Is it reassuring or frustrating to know that there is not a formula for sharing your faith with someone else? Why?

When Peter preached about the good news of Jesus in Acts 2:14-36, he was speaking to a Jewish audience and used language that would be very personal to their history as a nation. He quotes from the Hebrew Scriptures, specifically segments written by Joel and David that point to Jesus. He summarizes everything by saying, "Therefore let all the house of Israel know with certainty that God has made this Jesus, whom you crucified, both Lord and Messiah!" (v. 36). As a result, three thousand people came to faith in Jesus and were baptized that day.

With results like that, it might be tempting to think that Peter's message is the formula for evangelism that we should adopt. Quote a little Joel and David, point to Jesus, and tell people to repent and be baptized, and bingo: easy, repeatable evangelism. The problem is this is the only instance where Joel and David are mentioned in all the New Testament accounts of evangelism. The next evangelistic moment in Acts 3:11-26 reveals that Peter, speaking again to the Jewish people, mentions Abraham, Isaac, Jacob, the holy prophets, Moses, and Samuel as he described Jesus as the Holy and Righteous One. At this point, it might be tempting to suggest that evangelism always involves mentioning characters from the Old Testament. However, the next evangelistic account in Acts 4:8-12, records Peter as not mentioning any Old Testament names but rather references a recently healed beggar before concluding, "There is salvation in no one else, for there is no other name under heaven given to people, and we must be saved by it."

On and on it goes throughout the New Testament. It's always about Jesus, but it's never the same exact words that lead people to Jesus. This required much prayer, which is constantly mentioned as occurring among the early disciples, and it required being led by the Holy Spirit at all times.

Briefly describe how coming to know Jesus was different for you than for others in your family or small group.

The early disciples were being faithful to Jesus' last command to be "witnesses to Jesus" before He ascended to the right hand of God (see John 5:31-47). Knowing they couldn't do this on their own strength or wisdom, Jesus empowered every believer with the Holy Spirit (see Acts 2:4) and sent them out in the same way that God the Father had sent the Son (see John 20:21). This involved the words they spoke and the lives they lived. Their lives were compelling, drawing thousands to follow Jesus, despite tremendous persecution.

As you continue to follow the history of the early church through the Book of Acts and even in the New Testament Letters from Paul and others, you find that evangelism is always and only about Jesus. Luke summarized the disciples' passion in Acts 5:42, "Every day in the temple complex, and in various homes, they continued teaching and proclaiming the good news that Jesus is the Messiah." At the same time, different words were used to point to Jesus.

- Stephen summarizes much of the Old Testament to point to Jesus (Acts 7:2-53).
- Philip, through the power of the Spirit, healed many paralyzed people to point to Jesus (Acts 8:4-8).
- Peter boldly confronted Simon the sorcerer to point him to Jesus (Acts 8:9-24).
- Philip listened to and had compassion for the Ethiopian eunuch to point him to Jesus (Acts 8:26-40).
- Peter stepped outside his comfort zone to associate with a Gentile to point him to Jesus (Acts 10:25-48).
- Paul and Silas prayed and sang hymns in prison to point to Jesus (Acts 16:25-34).
- Paul reasoned with people in different ways to point to Jesus (Acts 17:1-34).

In summary, what would it look like for us today to point to Jesus everywhere we went? Because there is no formula to follow, it requires obedience by us continually putting into practice all that Jesus commanded. The more you cultivate in your own life a lifestyle of discipleship, the more equipped you'll be to point to Jesus in your conversations and in your actions.

What one thing can you do this week to share Christ through words or actions?

Think about a specific person in your life with whom God might be leading you to share the good news. What are some fears that have been stopping you? Pray and ask God to give you courage and opportunity to share. Remember it is our job to share the gospel, and it is the Holy Spirit's job to convict, compel, and change hearts.

ROMANS ROAD

One classic way to explain the gospel and God's plan of salvation is known as the "Romans Road." It uses a series of verses from the Book of Romans to explain the path to salvation through Christ. The Bible is clear that it is only through faith in Jesus that we are forgiven and reconciled to God. There are five essential elements of this message. Each of these steps is necessary to understand the one that follows. As you read through these verses, consider how you might explain each of these concepts to someone who is not yet a believer.

Who needs salvation:

[10] There is no one righteous, not even one.
[11] There is no one who understands;
there is no one who seeks God.
[12] All have turned away;
all alike have become useless.
There is no one who does what is good,
not even one.
ROMANS 3:10-12

For all have sinned and fall short of the glory of God.
ROMANS 3:23

Why we need salvation:

For the wages of sin is death, but the gift of God is eternal life in Christ Jesus our Lord.
ROMANS 6:23

How God provides salvation:

But God proves His own love for us in that while we were still sinners, Christ died for us!
ROMANS 5:8

How we receive salvation:

> [9] If you confess with your mouth, "Jesus is Lord," and believe in your heart that God raised Him from the dead, you will be saved. [10] One believes with the heart, resulting in righteousness, and one confesses with the mouth, resulting in salvation.
> **ROMANS 10:9-10**

> For everyone who calls on the name of the Lord will be saved.
> **ROMANS 10:13**

The result of salvation:

> Therefore, since we have been declared righteous by faith, we have peace with God through our Lord Jesus Christ.
> **ROMANS 5:1**

> Therefore, no condemnation now exists for those in Christ Jesus.
> **ROMANS 8:1**

> [38] For I am persuaded that not even death or life,
> angels or rulers,
> things present or things to come, hostile powers,
> [39] height or depth, or any other created thing
> will have the power to separate us
> from the love of God that is in Christ Jesus our Lord!
> **ROMANS 8:38-39**

Which step is the most difficult for you to describe? Explain your answer.

Which step would be the most challenging for your unbelieving friend to understand and accept? Explain your answer.

Where do you think most people in our culture get stuck and reject Jesus?

DISCIPLES PATH

If your group is continuing on the *Disciples Path* journey, choose your next study using the chart below or find other discipleship studies at *www.lifeway.com/goadults*

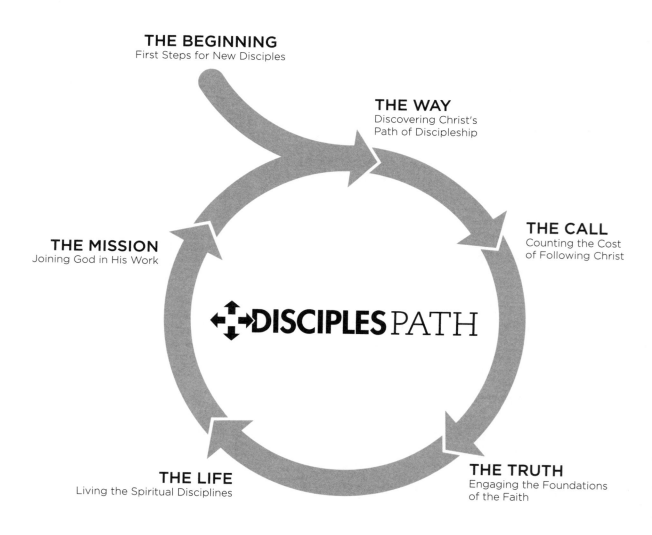

THE BEGINNING
First Steps for New Disciples

THE WAY
Discovering Christ's
Path of Discipleship

THE CALL
Counting the Cost
of Following Christ

THE MISSION
Joining God in His Work

DISCIPLES PATH

THE TRUTH
Engaging the Foundations
of the Faith

THE LIFE
Living the Spiritual Disciplines

TAKE THE NEXT STEP.

Disciples Path is a series of resources founded on Jesus' model of discipleship. Created by experienced disciple makers across the nation, it is an intentional path of transformational discipleship. While most small-group studies facilitate transformation through relationship and information, these disciple-making resources do it through the principles of modeling, practicing, and multiplying.

- Leaders model a biblical life.
- Disciples follow and practice from the leader.
- Disciples become disciple makers and multiply through *Disciples Path*.

Each of the six studies in the *Disciples Path* series has been written and approved by disciple makers for one-on-one settings as well as small groups. The series includes:

1. THE BEGINNING
Take the first step for a new believer and new disciple.

2. THE WAY
Walk through the Gospels and follow the journey of Jesus and the first disciples.

3. THE CALL
Gain a deeper understanding of what it means to follow Christ in everyday life.

4. THE TRUTH
Dive into the doctrinal truths of biblical discipleship.

5. THE LIFE
Take a deeper look at the essential disciplines and practices of following Christ.

6. THE MISSION
Get equipped for God's mission and discover your role in joining Him in the world.

To learn more or take the next step, visit *lifeway.com/disciplespath*

LEADER INSTRUCTIONS

As a group leader or mentor, you have a vital role in the process of discipleship—one that involves both blessing and responsibility. Keep in mind the following guidelines as you faithfully obey the Great Commission.

YOUR GOAL

Remember that your ultimate goal in the discipleship process is spiritual transformation. The best fruit for your efforts as a leader is spiritual growth that results in transformed hearts—both for you and for the disciples under your care.

Remember also that spiritual transformation is most likely to occur when a godly leader applies truth to the heart of a person while that person is in a teachable posture. As the leader, you have direct control over the first two of those conditions; you can also encourage and support disciples as they seek a teachable posture. Take advantage of those opportunities.

YOUR METHODS

Use the following suggestions as you work toward the goal of spiritual transformation.

- **Pray daily.** Studies have shown that leaders who pray every day for the disciples under their care see the most spiritual fruit during the discipleship process. Your ultimate goal is spiritual transformation; therefore, seek the Holy Spirit.

- **Teach information.** This resource contains helpful information on the basic elements of the Christian faith. During group discussions, you'll want to be familiar enough with the content to avoid reading each page verbatim. Highlighting key words or even creating your own bullet points will help you facilitate the time most effectively. Prepare in advance.

- **Seek conversation.** As you lead disciples through the material, seek to engage them in meaningful conversation. To help you, discussion questions have been provided throughout the group portion of each session. These questions provide an opportunity to pause and allow each disciple to react to the teaching. They also allow you as the disciple-maker an opportunity to gauge how each person is progressing along the path of discipleship.

- **Model practices.** Many disciples learn best by observing others. Therefore, each session of this resource includes opportunities for you to model the attributes, disciplines, and practices of a growing disciple of Jesus. Take advantage of these opportunities by intentionally showing disciples how to pray, interact with God's Word, worship God, and so on—and by inviting feedback and questions.

May God bless your efforts to guide others toward the blessing of new life through Christ and continued transformation through His Spirit.

NOTES

....

....

....

....

....

....

....

....

....

....

....

....

....

....

....

....

....

....

....

....

....

....

....

....

DISCIPLES PATH
Group Directory

Name: _____

Home Phone: _____

Mobile Phone: _____

Email: _____

Social Media: _____

Name: _____

Home Phone: _____

Mobile Phone: _____

Email: _____

Social Media: _____

Name: _____

Home Phone: _____

Mobile Phone: _____

Email: _____

Social Media: _____

Name: _____

Home Phone: _____

Mobile Phone: _____

Email: _____

Social Media: _____

Name: _____

Home Phone: _____

Mobile Phone: _____

Email: _____

Social Media: _____

Name: _____

Home Phone: _____

Mobile Phone: _____

Email: _____

Social Media: _____

Name: _____

Home Phone: _____

Mobile Phone: _____

Email: _____

Social Media: _____

Name: _____

Home Phone: _____

Mobile Phone: _____

Email: _____

Social Media: _____

Name: _____

Home Phone: _____

Mobile Phone: _____

Email: _____

Social Media: _____

Name: _____

Home Phone: _____

Mobile Phone: _____

Email: _____

Social Media: _____